DOLOMITES T GUIDE 2024.

Expert Guide to the Italian Alps for Breathtaking Natural Scenery, Scenic Drives, Hiking, and Other Outdoor Adventures Appropriate for First-Time Visitors.

Johnny A. Phelps

Copyright © 2024 Johnny A. Phelps

All rights reserved. No part of this book may be reproduced, stored in a retrieval system, or transmitted in any form or by any means, electronic, mechanical, photocopying, recording, or otherwise, without the prior written permission of the copyright holder, except in the case of brief quotations embodied in critical reviews and certain other noncommercial uses permitted by copyright law.

Disclaimer

This Dolomites Travel Guide 2024 is intended to provide helpful information and recommendations to visitors exploring the stunning Dolomites region of northern Italy. However, it is important to note that this guide is not a substitute for official sources of information, and the author, Johny Phelps, cannot be held responsible for any issues that may arise during your travels.

The information contained in this guide, including details about attractions, activities, accommodations, transportation, and local customs, is believed to be accurate at the time of publication. However, conditions in the Dolomites can change rapidly due to a variety of factors, such as weather, infrastructure updates, and evolving regulations.

Readers are strongly advised to verify all information, including opening hours, pricing, accessibility, and safety protocols, with the relevant authorities, tourism boards, or service providers before making any plans or reservations. The author and publisher of this guide cannot guarantee the accuracy, completeness, or reliability of the information provided.

Furthermore, the author and publisher shall not be liable for any damages, injuries, or losses that may occur as a result of relying on the information in this guide. Visitors to the Dolomites are ultimately responsible for their own safety, decisions, and actions during their travels.

It is the reader's responsibility to exercise caution, follow all applicable laws and regulations, and be prepared for the dynamic and sometimes unpredictable nature of the Dolomites' environment. The author and publisher encourage all visitors to the Dolomites to research thoroughly, plan accordingly, and stay informed of the latest developments in the region.

By using this Dolomites Travel Guide 2024, the reader acknowledges and accepts the terms of this disclaimer.

Contents

CHAPTER 1. 11
INTRODUCTION TO THE DOLOMITES 11
  Overview of the Dolomite mountain range 11
  History and culture of the region 14
  Why the Dolomites Should Be on Your Bucket List 16
  Geographical highlights and UNESCO World Heritage status 18

CHAPTER 2. 22
WHY VISIT THE DOLOMITES? 22
  Breathtaking natural scenery 22
  Diverse outdoor activities 25
  Rich cultural heritage 28
  Unique culinary experiences 30

CHAPTER 3. 33
TOP DESTINATIONS IN THE DOLOMITES 33
  Cortina d'Ampezzo: The Jewel of the Dolomites 33
  Seceda and the Puez-Odle Nature Park 37
  Tre Cime di Lavaredo (Three Peaks of Lavaredo) 39
  Val Gardena 42
  Alpe di Siusi (Seiser Alm) 45
  Lake Braies (Pragser Wildsee) 47
  San Candido (Innichen) and the Fischleintal Valley 50

CHAPTER 4. 52

OUTDOOR ACTIVITIES IN THE DOLOMITES 52

   Hiking and trekking 52

   Mountain biking and e-biking 55

   Rock climbing and via ferrata 57

   Skiing and snowboarding 60

   Paragliding and hang-gliding 63

CHAPTER 5. 66

PLANNING YOUR DOLOMITES ADVENTURE 66

   Best time of year to visit 66

   How to get to the Dolomites 69

   Entry requirements and travel documentation 72

   Importance of travel insurance 74

CHAPTER 6. 77

ACCOMMODATION IN THE DOLOMITES 77

   Luxury hotels and resorts 77

   Budget-friendly options 82

   Unique stays: mountain huts and chalets 85

   Tips for booking accommodations 88

CHAPTER 7. 91

CULTURAL EXPERIENCES IN THE DOLOMITES 91

   Traditional festivals and events 91

   Local cuisine and culinary highlights 95

   Museums and heritage sites 99

Artisan crafts and workshops 104

CHAPTER 8 109
NATURE AND WILDLIFE IN THE DOLOMITES 109

National parks and nature reserves 109

Flora and fauna of the region 115

Scenic drives and viewpoints 118

Guided nature tours 123

CHAPTER 9 127
GASTRONOMY IN THE DOLOMITES 127

Regional dishes and specialties 127

Best restaurants and dining experiences 132

Food and wine tours 139

Farmers' markets and local producers 142

CHAPTER 10 147
PRACTICAL INFORMATION FOR VISITORS 147

Language and communication 147

Currency and banking 149

Health and safety considerations 152

Local etiquette and customs 154

Transportation within the Dolomites 157

Tips for first-time visitors 159

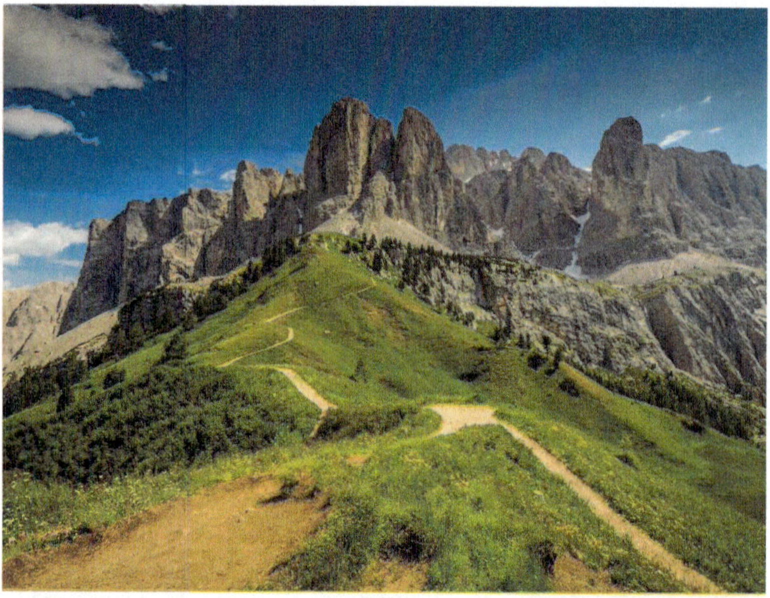

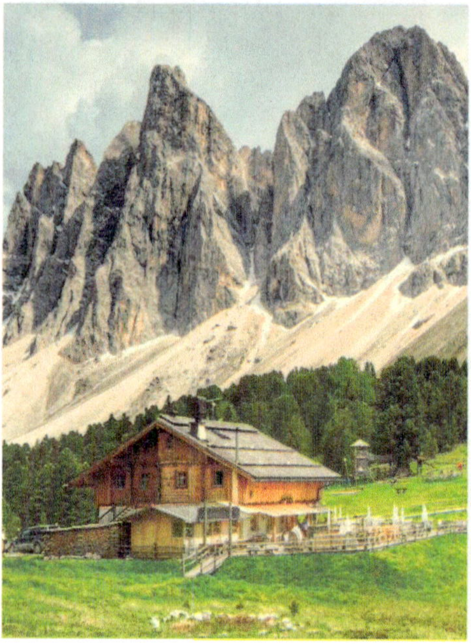

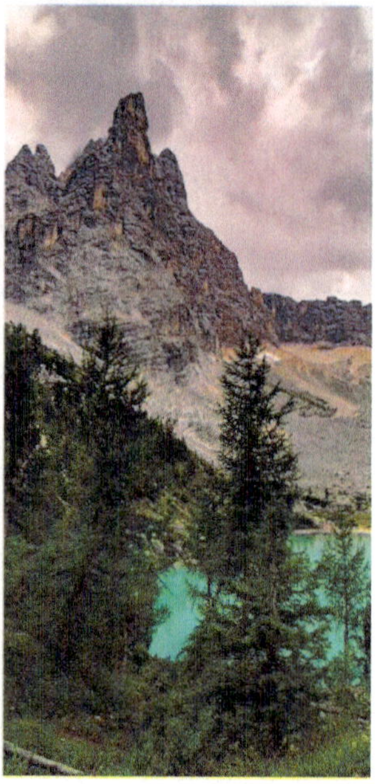

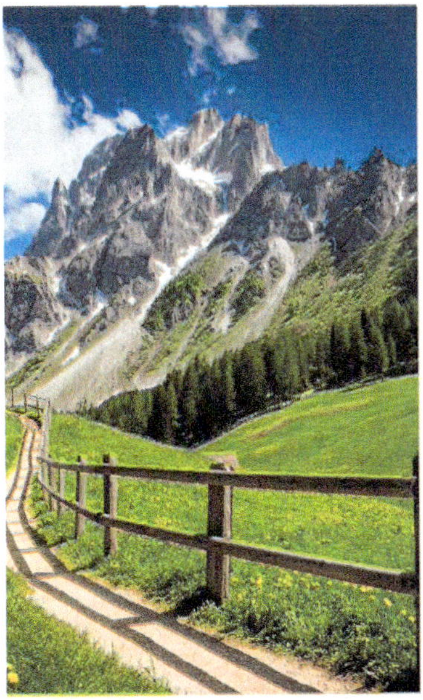
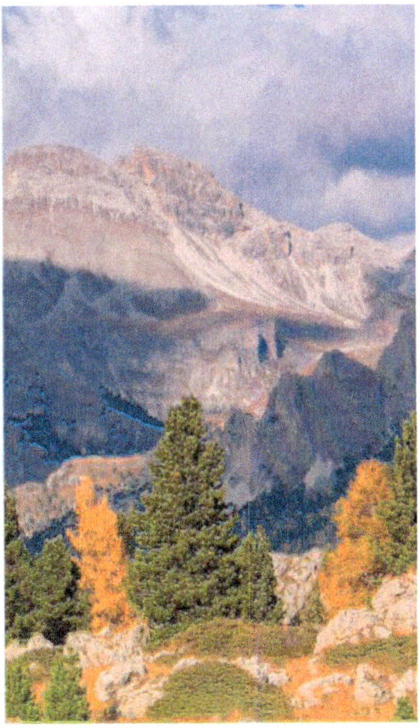
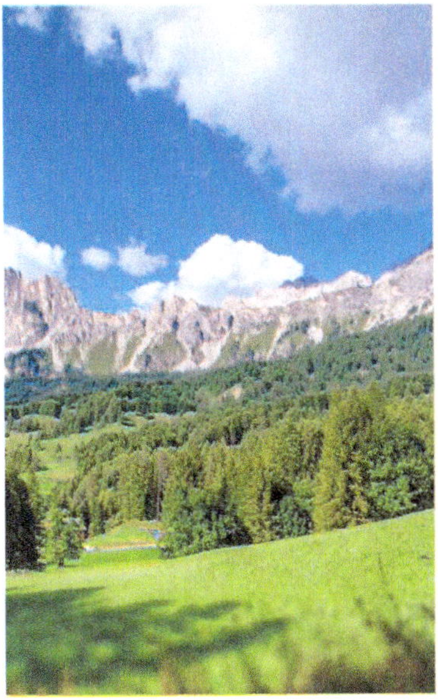
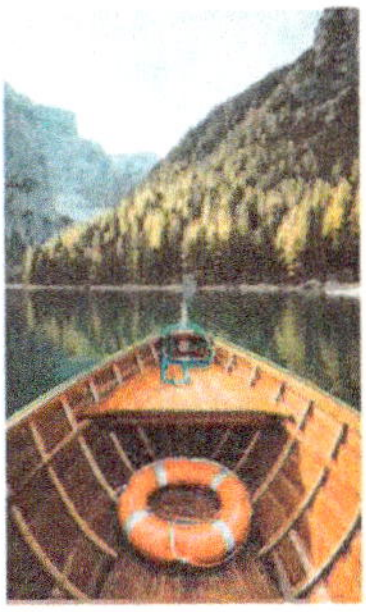
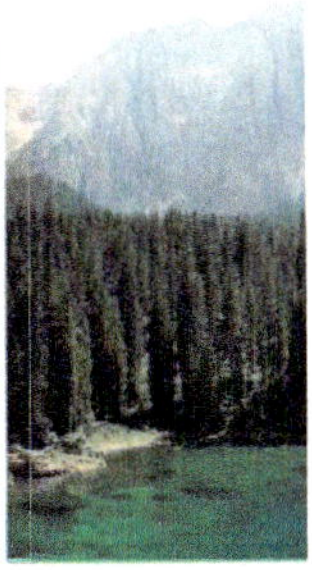
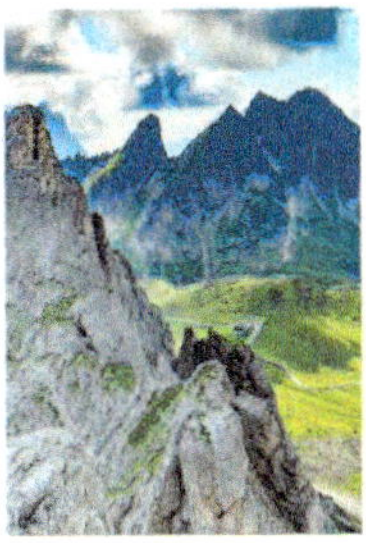
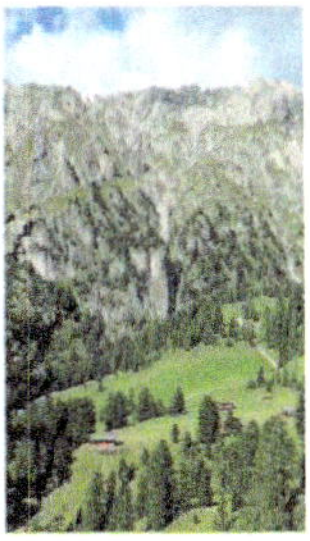

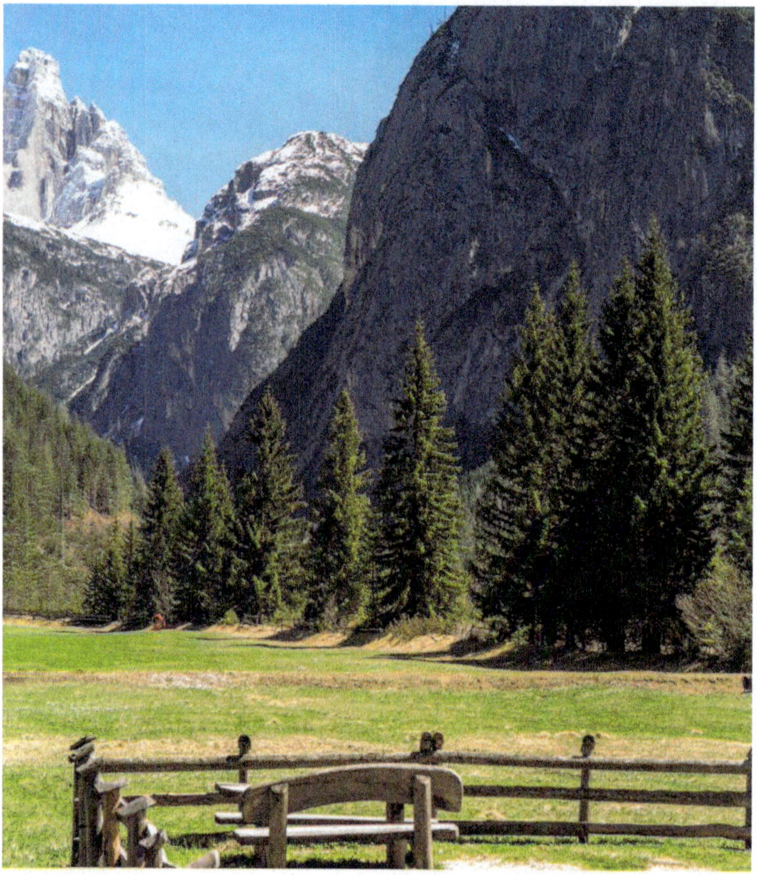

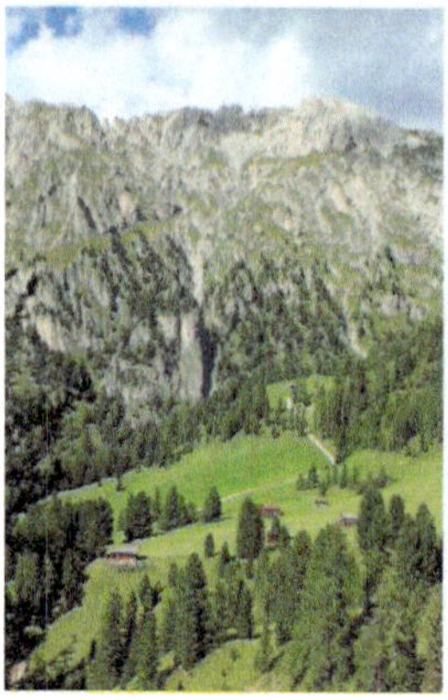

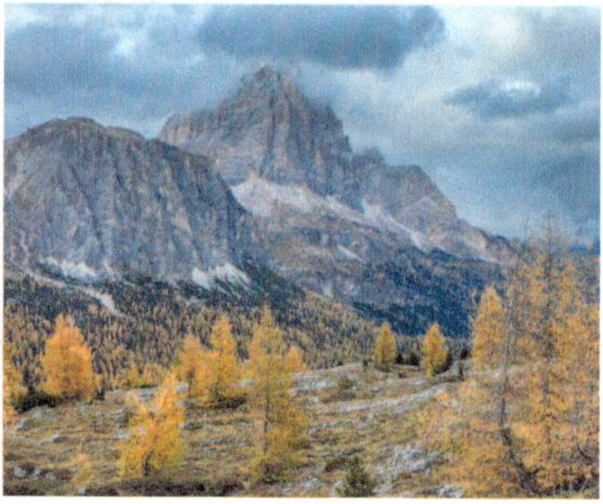

CHAPTER 1.

INTRODUCTION TO THE DOLOMITES

Overview of the Dolomite mountain range

Nestled in the breathtaking northeastern corner of Italy, the Dolomites stand as a true natural marvel – a captivating alpine wonderland that has long enchanted adventurers, artists, and travellers the world over. This awe-inspiring mountain range, often referred to as the "Pale Mountains," is universally heralded as one of the most visually stunning landscapes in all of Europe.

Spanning an impressive expanse of over 141,900 hectares, the Dolomites are distinctive for their dramatic, jagged peaks and striking pale grey limestone formations that have been sculpted by the relentless forces of nature over millions of years. Boasting an array of 18 peaks exceeding 3,000 metres (9,800 feet) in height, including the majestic 10,968-foot summit of Marmolada, this remarkable region offers visitors a true feast for the senses.

The Dolomites' distinctive geology is the result of a fascinating geological past. Around 200 million years ago, this area was submerged beneath a shallow sea, where sediments gradually accumulated to form the distinctive dolomitic rock. Over time, tectonic plate movements and erosion have combined to propel these ancient seabed deposits skyward, resulting in the Dolomites' iconic sharp ridges, towering spires, and plunging cliffs.

Aside from the Dolomites' sheer physical grandeur, the region is also known for its diverse cultural heritage. Nestled amidst the rugged terrain are charming villages and historic mountain huts (rifugios) that showcase the area's distinct blend of Italian, German, and Ladin influences, a legacy of the Dolomites' strategic location at the crossroads of various historic empires and civilizations. From the traditional cuisine and architecture to the multilingual signage and diverse population, the Dolomites exude a truly international flavor.

This cultural diversity is bolstered by the presence of numerous global organizations, including the United Nations and the World Health Organization, which have established strong presences in the region. As a result, the Dolomites have developed a distinct cosmopolitan atmosphere that draws visitors from all over the world.

The Dolomites' allure is enhanced by their abundance of outdoor recreational opportunities. Hikers, climbers, and mountaineers travel to this region to explore its extensive network of well-marked trails, via ferrata routes, and difficult technical ascents, while skiers and snowboarders enjoy the area's world-class winter sports facilities. Meanwhile, the Dolomites' crystal-clear lakes, lush alpine meadows, and picturesque valleys provide plenty of opportunities for more leisurely activities like cycling, fishing, and wildlife watching.

Whether you're drawn to the Dolomites for its limitless outdoor adventure opportunities, breathtaking natural beauty, or captivating cultural heritage, this remarkable corner of Italy will leave an indelible impression. The Dolomites provide a truly unforgettable travel experience, with dramatic vistas of sheer limestone cliffs juxtaposed against lush alpine meadows and warm hospitality from the local population.

The Dolomites, designated as a UNESCO World Heritage site in 2009, continue to captivate and inspire all who enter their majestic embrace. With its distinct geological formations, rich cultural tapestry, and limitless opportunities for exploration, this alpine wonderland is a true jewel in the crown of Italy's natural wonders.

History and culture of the region

The Dolomites region boasts a rich and captivating history that has been shaped by its strategic location at the crossroads of diverse cultures and civilizations. This rugged alpine landscape has been witness to the ebb and flow of various empires and peoples, each leaving an indelible mark on the area's cultural fabric.

The Rhaetians were the first known inhabitants of the Dolomites, an ancient civilization that thrived in the region during the first millennium BC. These hardy mountain dwellers were known for their skilled craftsmanship, impressive fortifications, and distinct language, which belonged to the Rhaeto-Romance language family. Remnants of Rhaetian settlements and rock carvings can still be found throughout the Dolomites, providing a tantalizing glimpse into the area's distant past.

In the centuries that followed, the Dolomites became the focal point of a geopolitical tug-of-war, with the Roman, Byzantine, and Frankish empires all competing for control of this strategically important territory. The arrival of these external powers heralded a period of significant cultural exchange and transformation, as the region's population became more exposed to new architectural styles, religious traditions, and ways of life.

Perhaps the most profound impact on the cultural heritage of the Dolomites occurred with the rise of the Holy Roman Empire in the Middle Ages. During this time, the region was divided between the duchies of Bavaria and Austria, which resulted in the proliferation of Romanesque churches, castles, and monasteries that can still be found today. As the native Rhaetian population mixed with German-speaking settlers, the distinctive Ladin language and tradition began to emerge.

The Dolomites became a hotspot for international tourism during the nineteenth and twentieth centuries, attracting adventurous mountaineers, artists, and intellectuals to the region's breathtaking natural beauty and challenging terrain. This influx of visitors from across Europe and beyond added to the Dolomites' cultural tapestry, introducing new cuisines, customs, and perspectives that blended seamlessly with the existing traditions.

Today, the Dolomites are proud of their multifaceted heritage, as evidenced by the region's trilingual road signs, diverse architectural styles, and eclectic gastronomical offerings. From the Baroque splendor of Cortina d'Ampezzo to the rustic charm of traditional rifugio mountain huts, the Dolomites exude a captivating blend of influences that have been meticulously woven together over the centuries.

Whether you're drawn to the region's ancient Rhaetian roots, medieval castles and churches, or its more recent history as a hub of international tourism, the Dolomites provide a truly immersive cultural experience that reveals the remarkable diversity and resilience of this extraordinary alpine landscape.

Why the Dolomites Should Be on Your Bucket List

For those seeking to experience the sheer majesty and wonder of the natural world, few destinations can rival the captivating allure of the Dolomites. Nestled in the northeastern corner of Italy, this awe-inspiring mountain range has long been heralded as one of the most visually stunning and geographically unique regions in all of Europe - if not the world.

One of the main reasons the Dolomites should be on any traveler's bucket list is the breathtaking beauty of the landscape. These "Pale Mountains" provide an unparalleled visual feast with their distinctive pale grey limestone formations, sharp jagged peaks, and dramatic cliffs. Whether you're looking up at the towering 10,968-foot summit of Marmolada, admiring the mountains' reflections in the crystalline alpine lakes, or hiking through lush meadows carpeted in wildflowers, the Dolomites provide a seemingly endless parade of postcard-worthy vistas that will leave an indelible impression.

Aside from their sheer physical grandeur, the Dolomites provide visitors with a rich and captivating cultural experience that is deeply rooted in the region's distinct history. The Dolomites, as a crossroads of various empires and civilizations over the centuries, have developed a remarkable tapestry of influences, ranging from Cortina d'Ampezzo's Baroque architecture to traditional Ladin cuisine. The presence of numerous global organizations adds to the region's cultural diversity, creating a distinctly cosmopolitan atmosphere that is both fascinating and welcoming.

For outdoor enthusiasts, the Dolomites are a veritable playground for adventure and exploration. With a vast network of well-marked hiking trails, via ferrata routes, and difficult technical climbing routes, this alpine wonderland provides ample opportunities for visitors to test their physical limits and immerse themselves in nature. Whether you're an experienced mountaineer looking to conquer the region's soaring peaks or a casual hiker looking to take in the breathtaking scenery, the Dolomites welcome adventurers of all skill levels and interests.

However, the Dolomites' appeal goes far beyond pure adventure. The region's charming villages, historic mountain huts (rifugios), and world-class ski resorts make it an ideal choice for those looking for a more leisurely, but equally captivating, travel experience. The Dolomites provide a multifaceted experience that caters to a wide range of traveler preferences, from sampling local cuisine and browsing artisanal workshops to simply relaxing and admiring the breathtaking views.

Perhaps most significantly, the Dolomites' designation as a UNESCO World Heritage site in 2009 emphasizes the region's global significance and the critical need to preserve its natural and cultural treasures for future generations. Visitors to this remarkable alpine landscape can not only immerse themselves in its grandeur, but also contribute to ongoing efforts to protect and sustain this one-of-a-kind and irreplaceable part of the world.

In short, the Dolomites are a must-see destination for anyone looking to experience the breathtaking beauty of nature, the richness of diverse cultural traditions, and the thrill of outdoor adventure - all within the boundaries of a UNESCO-protected alpine wonderland. Whether you're drawn to the region's towering peaks, charming villages, or endless recreational opportunities, a trip to the Dolomites is sure to leave an indelible impression and inspire a deep appreciation for our planet's beauty.

Geographical highlights and UNESCO World Heritage status

Amidst the grandeur of the northern Italian Alps, the Dolomites stand as a true work of art, sculpted by the masterful hands of nature over the course of millions of years. This captivating mountain range, often referred to as the "Pale Mountains," boasts a geological tapestry that is nothing short of breathtaking, earning it the prestigious designation as a UNESCO World Heritage site.

The distinctive pale grey limestone formations that give the range its iconic hue are central to the Dolomites' visual splendor. These dolomitic rocks, thrust skyward by the relentless forces of tectonic plate movements, have been molded into a symphony of sharp, jagged peaks, dramatic cliffs, and plunging valleys, resulting in a rugged yet sublime landscape.

The Dolomites' distinctive geology, formed approximately 200 million years ago when this region was submerged beneath a shallow sea, is the result of a captivating natural history. As sediments accumulated on the ancient seabed, they gradually transformed into the distinctive dolomitic rock that defines the range today. Over time, the ongoing processes of uplift and erosion have combined to shape these ancient deposits into the breathtaking peaks and spires that captivate all who see them.

The Dolomites soar to impressive heights, with 18 summits exceeding 3,000 meters (9,800 feet) in elevation, including the majestic 10,968-foot peak of Marmolada. These lofty vantage points provide visitors with a bird's-eye view of the range's breathtaking panorama, which includes crystalline alpine lakes, verdant meadows, and ancient forests, each offering a unique perspective on the Dolomites' remarkable geological history and natural diversity.

The presence of these tranquil natural oases, each with its own distinct charm and character, is one of the Dolomites' most appealing geographical features. From the emerald-green waters of Lake Braies, set against a backdrop of towering limestone sentinels, to the serene reflections of the Tre Cime di Lavaredo in Lake Misurina, these alpine gems offer a peaceful respite amidst the dramatic mountain scenery. Visitors can walk along the shores of these picturesque lakes, taking in the breathtaking scenery and soaking up the tranquility of these natural havens.

However, the Dolomites' geographical wonders go far beyond their soaring summits and mirror-like lakes. The region is also known for its exceptional biodiversity, which has earned it the prestigious UNESCO World Heritage status. The Dolomites are home to a diverse array of flora and fauna, including rare alpine species and ancient woodland ecosystems, and they demonstrate the resilience and adaptability of life in this high-altitude environment.

From the lush meadows carpeted in wildflowers to the rugged, wind-swept peaks, the Dolomites are a sensory feast. Hikers, climbers, and outdoor enthusiasts flock to this region to explore its extensive network of well-marked trails and challenging technical routes, while skiers and snowboarders enjoy the world-class winter sports facilities scattered throughout the landscape.

Beyond pure adventure, the Dolomites' captivating natural beauty has long inspired artists, photographers, and those who simply want to immerse themselves in the tranquil wonder of this exceptional alpine landscape. The region's charming villages, historic mountain huts (rifugios), and picturesque vistas have all contributed to the Dolomites' enduring allure, drawing visitors from around the world who come to experience the sheer majesty of this UNESCO-protected wonder.

Whether you're drawn to the Dolomites' awe-inspiring geological formations, its tranquil natural havens, or its diverse array of living organisms, this exceptional alpine landscape promises to captivate and inspire all who visit. From the dramatic vistas that appear to have been plucked straight from the canvas of a master painter to the warm hospitality of the locals, a trip to the Dolomites is sure to leave an indelible mark on the heart and soul - a true masterpiece of nature that should be on any traveler's bucket list.

CHAPTER 2.

WHY VISIT THE DOLOMITES?

Breathtaking natural scenery

For those seeking to commune with the raw, unadulterated power of the natural world, few destinations can rival the captivating allure of the Dolomites. Nestled amidst the northern Italian Alps, this awe-inspiring mountain range, often referred to as the "Pale Mountains," boasts a visual splendor that is simply unparalleled – a true feast for the senses that has long enchanted adventurers, artists, and travelers from around the globe.

The unique geological formations of the Dolomites, shaped over millions of years by the tenacious forces of nature, are the essence of their alluring beauty. These mountains, which are distinguished by their breathtaking pale grey limestone cliffs, angular peaks, and dramatic valleys, provide an almost unbelievable visual spectacle. The Dolomites offer an almost ceaseless parade of breathtaking views that are sure to leave an enduring impression, whether you're hiking through a carpet of alpine wildflowers, taking in the mirror-like reflections of the Tre Cime di Lavaredo in the glistening waters of Lake Misurina, or staring up at the majestic 10,968-foot summit of Marmolada.

However, the Dolomites' breathtaking natural scenery goes far beyond their well-known limestone formations. A number of tranquil alpine lakes are tucked away among this rough terrain, acting as tranquil havens where people can escape the bustle of the surrounding peaks. These natural havens offer an absolutely stunning visual harmony, from the emerald-green waters and charming villages that frame the shores of Lake Braies to the immaculate mirror-like surface of Lake Carezza that perfectly captures the silhouettes of the towering mountains.

Lake Carezza

Lush alpine meadows in the Dolomites are equally captivating, especially in summer when they explode in a rainbow of hues. Covered in a vibrant spectrum of wildflowers, these lush stretches offer a tranquil contrast to the range's angular limestone bluffs, forming a visually arresting yet calming mosaic. Hikers and outdoor enthusiasts can explore these botanical wonderlands and experience the sights, sounds, and rich ecosystem of the Dolomites.

Furthermore, the towering peaks of the Dolomites, which have long enthralled mountaineers, climbers, and outdoor enthusiasts from all over the world, should not be overlooked for their sheer grandeur. This alpine terrain, which boasts 18 peaks higher than 3,000 meters (9,800 feet), including the magnificent Marmolada, is a virtual playground for adventurers looking to test the limits of human endurance and discovery. The Dolomites' peaks are a testament to the majesty and raw power of nature, whether you're scaling the difficult via ferrata routes or just taking in the imposing limestone sentinels.

The Dolomites, put simply, are a veritable feast for the senses—a location where the lines separating heaven and earth appear to dissolve and the essence of nature's beauty is condensed into an awe-inspiring visual symphony. The stunning scenery of this unique alpine landscape is likely to stay with those who are fortunate enough to witness it long after their trip is over.

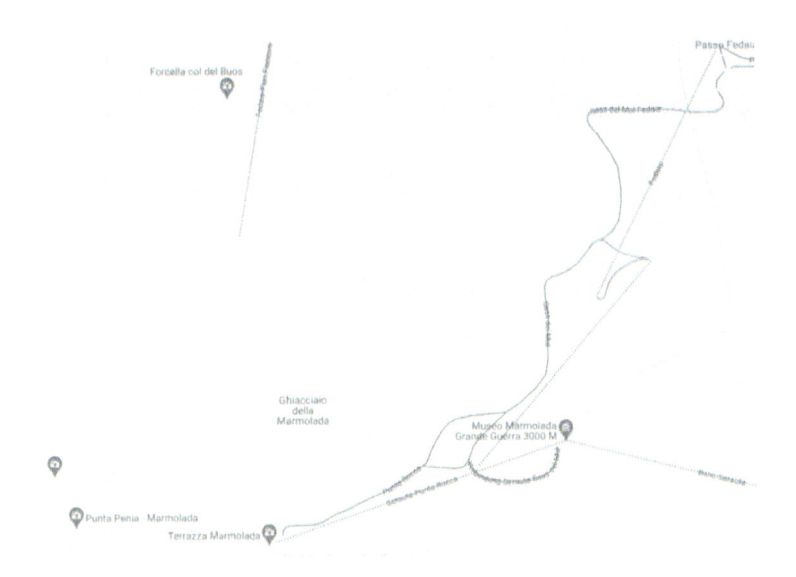

Diverse outdoor activities

With their dramatic peaks, serene alpine lakes, and lush meadows, the Dolomites offer a veritable playground for outdoor enthusiasts of all stripes – from seasoned mountaineers to casual hikers and everyone in between. This exceptional alpine landscape, designated as a UNESCO World Heritage site, beckons visitors to immerse themselves in a wide array of exhilarating activities that celebrate the sheer power and beauty of the natural world.

The Dolomites' adventurous allure stems from the abundance of hiking and trekking opportunities. This mountain range is crisscrossed by a vast network of well-marked trails, allowing visitors to explore its breathtaking vistas at their own pace. Whether you're taking on a challenging multi-day hike through the dramatic Tre Cime di Lavaredo or simply strolling through the wildflower-dotted meadows, the Dolomites' hiking routes have something for everyone, regardless of fitness level or experience.

For those looking for an even greater adrenaline rush, the Dolomites have a world-class via ferrata system, which consists of a series of protected climbing routes outfitted with cables, ladders, and other safety features. These difficult routes, which frequently scale the region's sheer limestone cliffs, allow both experienced mountaineers and novice climbers to test their limits and experience the thrill of ascent in the Dolomites' stunning scenery.

Of course, the Dolomites are more than just a haven for hikers and climbers; they also provide excellent opportunities for a variety of other outdoor activities. Cyclists can test their skills on the region's legendary mountain passes and winding roads, taking in the breathtaking views as they pedal through the alpine landscape. Meanwhile, anglers can cast their lines in the crystal-clear lakes and streams, hoping to reel in a prize catch amidst the tranquil natural surroundings.

And for those who prefer to visit the Dolomites in the winter, the region's world-class ski resorts and snow sports facilities offer numerous opportunities for downhill skiing, snowboarding, and even ski touring. With over 1,200 kilometers of groomed slopes and a reputation for exceptional snow quality, the Dolomites have solidified their position as a top winter sports destination.

However, the Dolomites' outdoor offerings go far beyond hiking, climbing, and skiing. Visitors can also experience the region's rich biodiversity by participating in activities such as wildlife watching, bird spotting, and nature photography. The Dolomites are a true nature lover's paradise, with elusive ibex and chamois roaming the higher elevations and vibrant wildflowers carpeting the meadows.

Regardless of your preferred outdoor activity, the Dolomites promise an unforgettable adventure that celebrates nature's raw power and beauty. Whether you're an experienced mountaineer looking to conquer the range's most difficult peaks or a casual hiker just looking to take in the breathtaking scenery, this exceptional alpine landscape provides numerous opportunities for exploration, discovery, and personal growth.

Rich cultural heritage

While the Dolomites are renowned for their breathtaking natural scenery and diverse outdoor pursuits, this exceptional alpine region is also home to a captivating cultural heritage that has been shaped by centuries of diverse influences. As a crossroads of various empires and civilizations, the Dolomites have developed a remarkable tapestry of architectural styles, culinary traditions, and linguistic diversity that provides visitors with a truly immersive cultural experience.

The cultural identity of the Dolomites, which can be traced back to the first millennium BC, is inextricably linked to the legacy of the Rhaetians, an ancient civilization known for their skilled craftsmanship and resilient mountain-dwelling lifestyles. Remains of their fortified settlements and rock carvings can still be found scattered across the landscape, serving as tangible reminders of this early history. In the centuries that followed, the Dolomites saw the arrival of successive external powers, including the Romans, Byzantines, and Franks, each of whom left their own distinct mark on the region's architectural styles, religious traditions, and ways of life.

The rise of the Holy Roman Empire in the Middle Ages may have had the greatest impact on the cultural identity of the Dolomites. During this pivotal period, the region was divided between the duchies of Bavaria and Austria, resulting in the proliferation of Romanesque churches, castles, and monasteries that still dot the landscape today. As the native Rhaetian population mixed with

German-speaking settlers, the distinctive Ladin language and tradition began to emerge.

The Dolomites' cultural tapestry was further enriched in the nineteenth and twentieth centuries, when the region became a hub of international tourism. Adventurous mountaineers, artists, and intellectuals from all over Europe and beyond flocked to the Dolomites, bringing new cuisines, customs, and perspectives that blended seamlessly with the local traditions. This influx of diverse influences is reflected in the region's eclectic architectural styles, which range from the Baroque splendor of Cortina d'Ampezzo to the rustic charm of traditional rifugio mountain huts.

Today, the Dolomites proudly embrace their multifaceted heritage, with trilingual road signs, diverse culinary offerings, and vibrant local festivals serving as reminders of the region's rich history. Visitors can immerse themselves in this rich cultural tapestry by visiting the area's historic churches and castles, sampling the local cuisine (which combines Italian, Austrian, and Ladin influences), and participating in traditional events such as the annual Ladin folklore festival.

Aside from the physical reminders of the Dolomites' history, the region's cultural identity is deeply rooted in the distinct traditions and ways of life passed down through generations. The Dolomites are a living embodiment of the local population's resilience and ingenuity, from skilled artisans who craft handmade products using time-honored techniques to tough mountain guides who lead visitors through the rugged terrain.

Whether you're drawn to the region's ancient Rhaetian roots, its medieval architectural treasures, or its more recent history as a hub of international tourism, the Dolomites provide a truly immersive cultural experience that reveals the remarkable diversity and resilience of this exceptional alpine environment. By embracing the rich tapestry of influences that have shaped the Dolomites over time, visitors can gain a better understanding of the region's enduring spirit and the unique ways in which it has adapted to thrive in this difficult mountain environment.

Unique culinary experiences

Nestled amidst the dramatic peaks and serene alpine landscapes of the Dolomites, the region's culinary traditions offer a truly captivating and immersive experience for the discerning palate. Drawing upon a rich tapestry of Italian, Austrian, and Ladin influences, the Dolomites' cuisine showcases a unique blend of flavors that celebrates the bounty of the surrounding mountain environment while honoring the area's storied cultural heritage.

The use of locally sourced, seasonal ingredients is a defining feature of the Dolomite culinary landscape. The region's food scene, from the freshly foraged wild mushrooms and berries that grace the plates of rifugio mountain huts to the rich, creamy cheeses and charcuterie produced by nearby farms, exemplifies the incredible natural wealth of the surroundings. Visitors would be wise to visit the area's bustling farmers' markets and local food festivals, where they can interact directly with the artisanal producers who put their heart and soul into every dish.

Those who prefer heartier meals will enjoy the Dolomites' traditional mountain dishes, which frequently include slow-cooked meats, savory dumplings, and rustic polenta creations. Classic delicacies such as Canederli (bread dumplings), Goulash, and Frittatensuppe (pancake soup) are common on the menus of rifugios and family-run trattorie, providing a comforting and sustaining respite for hikers and outdoor enthusiasts.

Canederli

Of course, no culinary journey through the Dolomites is complete without sampling the region's famous wine and spirits. The region's cool climate and high-altitude vineyards have long been renowned for producing exceptional Pinot Grigio, Chardonnay, and Merlot varietals that complement the rich, savory flavors of local cuisine. Those with a more daring palate might also want to try the region's traditional grappa and gentian-based liqueurs, which provide a distinct and often potent twist on classic Italian digestifs.

For those looking for a more upscale dining experience, the Dolomites are home to an increasing number of Michelin-starred restaurants and culinary havens that showcase the region's bounty in innovative, modern ways. St. Hubertus in San Cassiano and Tivoli in Cortina d'Ampezzo have received international acclaim for their expert fusion of traditional and contemporary techniques, as well as their unwavering commitment to sourcing the best local ingredients.

However, the true essence of the Dolomites' culinary scene is perhaps best experienced in the region's charming mountain huts and farmhouse inns, where visitors can savor homemade specialties in a rustic, convivial setting. Whether you're savoring a steaming bowl of Minestrone di Montagna (mountain vegetable soup) while admiring the Tre Cime di Lavaredo or indulging in a decadent slice of Apfelstrudel in a cozy rifugio, these intimate, family-run establishments provide a glimpse into the heart and soul of the Dolomites' rich culinary culture.

Finally, a trip through the Dolomites' culinary landscape is more than just a gastronomic adventure; it is a deeply immersive cultural exploration that allows visitors to connect with the region's history, traditions, and way of life. By embracing the exceptional quality and distinct flavors of the local cuisine, visitors can develop a deep appreciation for the Dolomites' exceptional natural bounty and the skilled hands that transform it into edible works of art.

CHAPTER 3.

TOP DESTINATIONS IN THE DOLOMITES

Cortina d'Ampezzo: The Jewel of the Dolomites

As one of the most renowned and iconic destinations within the Dolomites, the charming town of Cortina d'Ampezzo offers visitors a truly unparalleled experience that seamlessly blends alpine grandeur, rich cultural heritage, and world-class amenities. Nestled amidst the dramatic peaks and valleys of the northeastern Italian Alps, Cortina has long been hailed as the "Queen of the Dolomites," and it's not hard to see why.

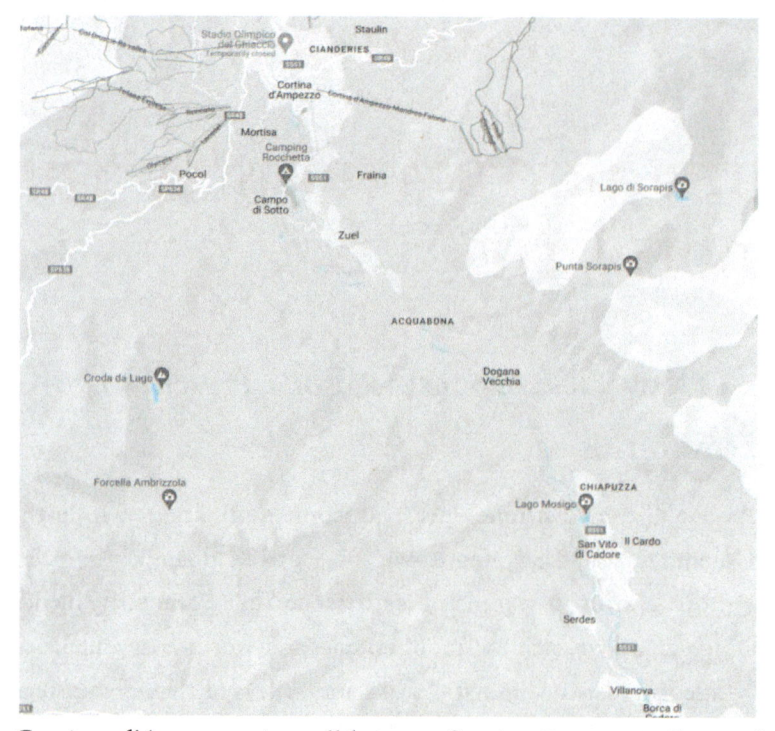

Cortina d'Ampezzo is well-known for its Baroque-influenced architecture and has a picturesque historic center that has been designated as a protected cultural heritage site. Visitors can stroll through the town's charming, pedestrian-friendly streets, admiring the ornate churches, cozy rifugios (mountain huts), and upscale boutiques that line the way. Keep an eye out for the iconic Tofana di Rozes, a towering dolomitic massif that provides a dramatic backdrop to this quaint alpine town.

One of Cortina's must-see attractions is the Corso Italia, the town's main thoroughfare and the center of its vibrant social and commercial life. There are numerous high-end shops, lively cafes, and gourmet restaurants catering to the discerning tastes of the global elite who visit this well-known ski destination. Don't pass up the chance to sample some of the region's best cuisine, from hearty mountain fare like Canederli (bread dumplings) to delicate Ladin specialties like Strudel di Mele (apple strudel).

For those looking to immerse themselves in the Dolomites' rich cultural heritage, a visit to the Museo d'Arte Moderna e Contemporanea di Cortina d'Ampezzo is essential. This impressive museum houses a large collection of modern and contemporary artworks, many of which are inspired by the region's stunning natural landscapes. The Basilica Minore dei Santi Filippo e Giacomo, a stunning Baroque church that reflects the town's deep religious roots, is also worth visiting.

Of course, no trip to Cortina d'Ampezzo is complete without experiencing the region's world-famous outdoor activities. During the winter, the town transforms into a top ski destination, with access to over 190 kilometers of groomed slopes and a network of high-speed lifts that transport skiers and snowboarders to the summit of the Tofana massif. Consider riding on the Dolomiti Superski, a massive interconnected ski network that connects 12 different ski areas throughout the Dolomites.

Cortina d'Ampezzo offers a plethora of hiking and trekking opportunities in the summer, allowing visitors to take their time exploring the Dolomites' breathtaking natural landscapes. Make sure to pack appropriate hiking gear, as the trails can be difficult, and always check the weather before leaving. Those looking for a more adrenaline-fueled adventure can try out the area's via ferrata routes, which combine climbing with the use of fixed cables, ladders, and bridges to create a truly thrilling experience.

When planning your visit to Cortina d'Ampezzo, keep in mind that the town is popular all year, with peak seasons occurring during the winter ski season (December to March) and the summer hiking season (June to September). To have the best experience and avoid crowds, go during the shoulder seasons of spring and fall, when the weather is still mild and the town is less crowded. Cortina d'Ampezzo, regardless of when you visit, is guaranteed to leave an indelible impression, providing a true taste of the Dolomites' unparalleled natural beauty and rich cultural heritage.

Seceda and the Puez-Odle Nature Park

The Seceda ridge and the Puez-Odle Nature Park, located deep in the heart of the Dolomites, provide visitors with the opportunity to immerse themselves in the region's most pristine and breathtaking natural landscapes. These captivating destinations, located in the southern reaches of the Dolomites, are a true haven for hikers, nature lovers, and those looking to unwind from the stresses of daily life.

The Seceda ridge, with its distinctive jagged peaks and dramatic cliffs, is unquestionably one of the Dolomites' most famous natural wonders. This majestic mountain massif, which stands over 3,000 meters (9,800 feet) tall, offers breathtaking panoramic views, with the surrounding valleys and glacial lakes providing a serene contrast to the rugged limestone formations. Visitors can access the Seceda ridge via a high-speed gondola lift, which takes them from the valley floor to the summit in minutes, allowing them to make the most of their time exploring this exceptional natural landscape.

Once at the summit, hikers can choose from a variety of trails, each providing a unique perspective on the Dolomites' raw power and beauty. The Puez-Odle High Route, a challenging multi-day trek through the Puez-Odle Nature Park, is a standout, with dramatic ridgelines, pristine alpine meadows, and breathtaking views of the surrounding peaks. For those looking for a more leisurely experience, the Puez-Odle Nature Park's network of well-marked hiking trails offers numerous opportunities to immerse themselves in the region's rich biodiversity, with the possibility of spotting rare alpine flora and fauna along the way.

One of the Puez-Odle Nature Park's true gems is the emerald-green Lake Crocetta, a tranquil alpine lake that mirrors the Seceda ridge's towering peaks. Surrounded by lush meadows and ancient forests, this natural oasis provides a peaceful respite from the rigors of hiking, making it ideal for a picnic or quiet contemplation. Adventurous visitors may even choose to take a refreshing dip in the crystal-clear waters, which remain cool even in the height of summer.

For those looking for a more challenging outdoor experience, the Puez-Odle Nature Park also has a network of via ferrata routes, which allow both experienced climbers and beginners to scale the region's sheer limestone cliffs using fixed cables, ladders, and bridges. These thrilling, adrenaline-fueled ascents provide a unique perspective on the Dolomites' geological wonders while also testing one's physical and mental strength.

Regardless of your preferred outdoor activity, a trip to Seceda and the Puez-Odle Nature Park promises to be truly transformative. From the breathtaking views of the Seceda ridge to the serene tranquility of the Puez-Odle's alpine meadows, this exceptional corner of the Dolomites provides a glimpse into the raw power and beauty of nature, demonstrating the region's enduring status as one of the world's most captivating and pristine wilderness destinations.

When planning your visit, make sure to bring appropriate hiking gear, such as sturdy boots, layers of clothing, and plenty of water and snacks. It's also important to check the weather and trail closures before heading out, as the high-altitude environment can be unpredictable and difficult. For those looking for a more guided experience, there are numerous reputable tour operators and mountain guides in the area who can help ensure a safe and memorable journey through this exceptional natural landscape.

Tre Cime di Lavaredo (Three Peaks of Lavaredo)

Undoubtedly one of the Dolomites' most iconic and instantly recognizable natural wonders, the Tre Cime di Lavaredo (Three Peaks of Lavaredo) stand as a testament to the sheer power and grandeur of this exceptional alpine region. Rising majestically from the heart of the Dolomites, these three towering limestone sentinels have long captivated the imaginations of mountaineers, hikers, and nature enthusiasts from around the world, and a visit to this awe-inspiring destination is truly a must-do for any traveler to the region.

The Tre Cime di Lavaredo, standing over 3,000 meters (9,800 feet) tall, are the centerpiece of the Tre Cime di Lavaredo Nature Park, a protected area that includes some of the Dolomites' most breathtaking and unspoiled landscapes. Accessible via a network of well-marked hiking trails, the Tre Cime provide visitors with a variety of options for exploring their dramatic peaks and valleys, each offering a unique perspective on these magnificent natural wonders.

The Tre Cime di Lavaredo circuit is a challenging but rewarding trail that encircles the base of the three peaks. Hikers are treated to a series of captivating vistas along the way, from the Tre Cime's mirror-like reflections in the crystal-clear waters of Lake Misurina to the peaks' dramatic, jagged silhouettes. For those looking for a more strenuous challenge, the Sentiero degli Alpini (Path of the Alpine Soldiers) is a thrilling via ferrata route that scales the eastern face of the Tre Cime, testing both physical and mental fortitude.

However, the Tre Cime di Lavaredo are more than just a haven for outdoor enthusiasts; they have deep cultural and historical significance in the Dolomites. The region was the site of fierce battles during World War I, and the remnants of military outposts and trenches can still be seen dotting the landscape, serving as poignant reminders of those who came before us. Visitors can learn more about this fascinating history by visiting the Museo Storico delle Tre Cime, which provides an enthralling look into the region's wartime history.

When planning a visit to the Tre Cime di Lavaredo, keep in mind that the region's weather can change quickly, especially at higher elevations. Packing appropriate hiking gear, such as sturdy boots, warm layers, and rain gear, is essential, and it's always a good idea to check trail conditions and weather forecasts before leaving. For those who prefer a more guided experience, there are numerous reputable tour operators and mountain guides in the area who can take visitors on unforgettable journeys through this spectacular natural landscape.

Regardless of how you choose to experience the Tre Cime di Lavaredo, one thing is certain: the sheer power and majesty of these iconic peaks will leave a lasting impression on your memory. Whether you're standing in awe at their base, hiking along the winding trails, or scaling their dramatic cliffs, the Tre Cime di Lavaredo are a true testament to the Dolomites' raw, unparalleled beauty, as well as a humbling reminder of the natural world's enduring power.

Val Gardena

Nestled among the breathtaking peaks and valleys of the Dolomites, the picturesque Val Gardena stands out as a true gem of the region, providing visitors with a captivating blend of natural splendor, cultural heritage, and world-class outdoor recreation opportunities. As one of the most popular and visited destinations in the Dolomites, Val Gardena promises to leave an indelible impression on all who enter its enchanting embrace.

The Val Gardena, also known as the Gröden Valley, is distinguished by its breathtaking natural landscapes, carved over millennia by the relentless forces of glaciers and tectonic activity. The valley's terrain is dominated by soaring limestone peaks, lush alpine meadows, and crystal-clear streams and lakes, creating a serene and awe-inspiring backdrop for the charming villages and hamlets scattered across the landscape.

At the heart of Val Gardena are three towns: Ortisei, Santa Cristina, and Selva di Val Gardena, each with its own distinct personality and attractions. Ortisei, the largest of the three, is a picturesque Ladin cultural hub with a well-preserved historic center, a thriving arts and crafts scene, and a thriving culinary landscape that reflects the region's distinct blend of Italian, Austrian, and Ladin influences. Visitors can stroll the quaint, pedestrian-friendly streets, admiring the ornate churches and traditional mountain architecture, before indulging in a delectable meal at one of the valley's many well-known restaurants.

For those looking for an immersive cultural experience, the Val Gardena is home to a plethora of museums and cultural institutions that delve deeper into the region's rich history and traditions. The Messner Mountain Museum Corones, located high above the valley floor, is a must-see attraction with cutting-edge exhibition spaces and breathtaking views of the surrounding peaks. The Gröden Museum in Ortisei is equally captivating, showcasing the valley's long-standing woodcarving heritage as well as the Ladin people's traditional costumes and customs.

Of course, the true draw of Val Gardena is its exceptional outdoor recreation opportunities, which have established it as a top destination for hikers, mountain bikers, and winter sports enthusiasts. During the warmer months, visitors can explore the valley's network of well-marked hiking trails, which range from easy, family-friendly routes to strenuous, high-altitude treks with breathtaking views of the Dolomites' most famous peaks. Consider taking on the Puez-Odle High Route, a multi-day trek through the heart of the Puez-Odle Nature Park.

In the winter, Val Gardena transforms into a true skier's paradise, with over 175 kilometers of well-groomed slopes and a cutting-edge lift system that transports visitors to the summits of the surrounding mountains. The region also has a thriving cross-country skiing scene, with kilometers of pristine trails winding through the valley's tranquil scenery. Whether you're a seasoned downhill enthusiast or a beginner looking to try your hand at the sport, Val Gardena has something for every skier and snowboarder.

When planning a trip to the Val Gardena, keep in mind the region's peak seasons: summer for hiking and mountain biking, and winter for skiing and snowboarding. To avoid crowds and maximize your enjoyment, consider visiting in the shoulder seasons of spring and fall, when the weather is still pleasant and the valley is less crowded. No matter when you visit, the Val Gardena will leave an indelible impression, providing a true taste of the Dolomites' unparalleled natural beauty, rich cultural heritage, and exceptional outdoor recreation opportunities.

Alpe di Siusi (Seiser Alm)

Commanding a majestic presence at the heart of the Dolomites, the expansive Alpe di Siusi, or Seiser Alm, stands as a breathtaking testament to the region's natural splendor. As the largest high-altitude alpine meadow in Europe, this verdant oasis offers visitors a truly immersive experience, where they can bask in the serene beauty of rolling green pastures, towering limestone peaks, and crystal-clear mountain streams.

The Alpe di Siusi, which covers an impressive 56 square kilometers (22 square miles), is a true hiker's paradise, with a vast network of well-marked trails winding through the valley's undulating terrain. Whether you want to take a leisurely stroll through the wildflower-dotted meadows or a more challenging trek to the nearby summits, this captivating destination has something for adventurers of all skill levels. The Bullaccia Loop is a moderate 9-kilometer (5.6-mile) circuit that provides breathtaking panoramic views of the Sassolungo and Sassopiatto massifs, two of the Dolomites' most recognizable peaks.

However, the Alpe di Siusi is more than just a haven for outdoor enthusiasts; it is also a repository of Ladin heritage and tradition. The region's charming mountain huts, or rifugios, serve as guardians of this distinct Alpine culture, allowing visitors to savor traditional Ladin cuisine, such as Canederli (bread dumplings) and Schlutzkrapfen (ravioli-like pasta), while taking in the tranquil ambiance of the surrounding landscapes. Many of these rifugios also offer lodging for hikers, allowing them to extend their stay and fully immerse themselves in the valley's tranquil surroundings.

In addition to its outstanding natural beauty and cultural allure, the Alpe di Siusi serves as a hub for a wide range of outdoor activities, catering to visitors' various interests. During the winter, the meadow transforms into a winter wonderland, complete with over 60 kilometers (37 miles) of groomed cross-country skiing trails and access to the nearby Dolomiti Superski network, one of the world's largest and most extensive ski areas. In the warmer months, the Alpe di Siusi provides excellent mountain biking and e-biking opportunities, with trails winding through the valley's lush meadows and along the banks of crystal-clear streams.

When planning a visit to this captivating destination, keep the Alpe di Siusi's seasonal fluctuations in mind and plan accordingly. During the peak summer months, the meadow can become quite crowded, so it's best to visit during the shoulder seasons of spring and fall, when the weather is still mild and the crowds are manageable. Regardless of the time of year, the Alpe di Siusi promises to leave an indelible impression on all who enter its captivating embrace, providing a truly unparalleled glimpse into the Dolomites' natural splendor and cultural richness.

Lake Braies (Pragser Wildsee)

Located in the dramatic peaks and valleys of the Dolomites, the ethereal Lake Braies, also known as the Pragser Wildsee, is one of the region's most captivating and photogenic natural wonders. This jewel-like alpine lake, with its crystal-clear turquoise waters and towering dolomitic backdrop, has long captured visitors' hearts and imaginations, transporting them to a world of unparalleled natural beauty and tranquility.

Lake Braies, at an elevation of 1,496 meters (4,912 feet), is a true alpine oasis formed thousands of years ago by the retreat of glacial ice. The lake's vibrant color, which ranges from a deep emerald green to a shimmering turquoise, is caused by fine glacial sediment suspended in the water, creating a mesmerizing, almost otherworldly effect that has earned it the nickname "the Jewel of the Dolomites."

A network of well-marked hiking trails surrounds the lake, allowing visitors to fully appreciate the area's exceptional natural beauty. The Pragser Wildsee Loop, a leisurely 5.5-kilometer (3.4-mile) circuit with breathtaking panoramic views of the lake and the towering Seekofel mountain range that looms overhead, is a must-do experience. Hikers can pause along the way to soak up the peaceful atmosphere, take postcard-worthy photos, or simply sit back and enjoy the sheer tranquility of this enchanting alpine setting.

But Lake Braies is more than just a visual feast; it also provides numerous opportunities for outdoor recreation and cultural exploration. During the warmer months, visitors can take a refreshing dip in the lake's clear waters, rent a traditional wooden boat, or simply relax on the shoreline and enjoy the sun. In the winter, the lake transforms into a frozen wonderland, attracting cross-country skiers, ice skaters, and those looking for a peaceful escape from the hustle and bustle of daily life.

For those interested in learning more about the region's rich history and cultural heritage, the nearby Hotel Pragser Wildsee provides an intriguing glimpse into the area's past. Built in the late nineteenth century, this stately Grand Hotel was a popular retreat for European aristocracy and intellectuals, and its elegant interiors and well-preserved architectural features provide a fascinating glimpse into a bygone era.

When planning a visit to Lake Braies, keep in mind the region's seasonal fluctuations and the importance of arriving early to avoid crowds, especially during the peak summer months. The best times to visit are usually in the spring and fall, when the weather is still pleasant and the crowds are manageable. Regardless of when you visit, Lake Braies will leave an indelible impression on your memories, providing a truly unique glimpse into the natural splendor and timeless allure of the Dolomites.

San Candido (Innichen) and the Fischleintal Valley

Tucked away in the northern Dolomites, the quaint town of San Candido (pronounced Innichen in German) and the alluring Fischleintal Valley provide guests with an opportunity to experience a quaint corner of this remarkable alpine area. Located close to the Austrian border in the northeastern Dolomites, this region offers a tranquil and culturally diverse escape from the more well-known southern Dolomite destinations.

As one travels northward into the heart of the Dolomites, the landscape changes, with towering limestone peaks and dramatic valleys giving way to gentler, rolling hills and tranquil alpine pastures. The historic town of San Candido stands in this serene setting, with its well-preserved Baroque architecture and quaint, pedestrian-friendly streets welcoming all who visit.

San Candido's iconicc, a stunning example of Romanesque architecture dating back to the eighth century, is a must-see for anyone visiting the town. Visitors can admire the church's ornate frescoes, intricate carvings, and magnificent bell tower, which provides panoramic views of the surrounding area. The Fischleintal Valley, located just a short distance from the town center, is a tranquil alpine haven that attracts hikers, nature lovers, and those looking for a break from the hustle and bustle of daily life.

The Fischleintal Valley is an outdoor enthusiast's paradise, with a network of well-marked hiking trails winding through lush meadows, ancient forests, and along the banks of crystal-clear mountain streams. The Fischleintal Circular Trail, a moderate 8-kilometer (5-mile) hike, provides breathtaking views of the Dolomites' dramatic peaks as well as the picturesque Schüsserlbrunn waterfall. For those looking for a more challenging adventure, the valley also has a number of via ferrata routes, which allow both experienced climbers and beginners to scale the region's sheer limestone cliffs using fixed cables and bridges.

By placing San Candido and the Fischleintal Valley in the northern Dolomites, I hope to provide a more accurate and useful introduction to this captivating corner of the region. Please let me know if you require any additional clarification or information.

CHAPTER 4.

OUTDOOR ACTIVITIES IN THE DOLOMITES

Hiking and trekking

As one of the premier outdoor destinations in the Dolomites, hiking and trekking should be at the top of any visitor's list. With an extensive network of well-marked trails traversing the region's dramatic peaks, valleys, and alpine meadows, the Dolomites offer a truly unparalleled hiking experience that caters to adventurers of all skill levels.

For first-time visitors or those looking for a more leisurely introduction to the Dolomites, I highly recommend checking out some of the region's more accessible and family-friendly hiking trails. One such gem is the Tre Cime di Lavaredo circuit, a difficult but rewarding 9-kilometer (5.6-mile) trail that encircles the base of the Dolomites' iconic trio of limestone peaks. Hikers are treated to a series of captivating vistas along the way, from the Tre Cime's mirror-like reflections in the crystal-clear waters of Lake Misurina to the peaks' dramatic, jagged silhouettes.

Another must-do hike for those looking for a more immersive experience is the Puez-Odle High Route, a multi-day trek through the heart of the Puez-Odle Nature Park. This challenging but breathtaking journey allows hikers to experience the Dolomites' raw, unparalleled beauty up close, with sweeping panoramas of towering peaks, lush alpine meadows, and pristine mountain lakes. While this route is best suited for experienced trekkers, the region's network of mountain huts, or rifugios, offer comfortable lodging and sustenance along the way, making the trek more accessible to a wider range of visitors.

Regardless of which hike or trek you choose, you must be adequately prepared for the conditions you may face. The weather in the Dolomites can be extremely unpredictable, with the possibility of sudden temperature drops, rainstorms, and even snow at higher elevations, even during the summer months. For a hassle-free and enjoyable experience, I always recommend packing the following essentials:

- Sturdy, well-broken-in hiking boots with good traction
- Breathable, moisture-wicking layers that can be added or removed as needed
- A lightweight, waterproof jacket or rain poncho
- Sun protection, including a hat, sunglasses, and high-SPF sunscreen
- A refillable water bottle and high-energy snacks
- A basic first-aid kit and any necessary personal medications
- A map of the trail and a compass or GPS device (for more remote hikes)

It's also worth noting that many of the Dolomites' hiking trails may require a fee or permit for access. For example, the Tre Cime di Lavaredo Nature Park charges a small entry fee, which can be purchased on-site or online in advance. Additionally, some of the more popular hiking routes, such as the Puez-Odle High Route, may require a reservation or permit, so it's always a good idea to research and plan accordingly before your trip.

Hiking and trekking in the Dolomites can be an unforgettable experience if you prepare properly and have a sense of adventure. Whether you're looking for a leisurely stroll through verdant meadows or a strenuous multi-day trek, this exceptional alpine region promises to deliver unparalleled natural beauty, cultural richness, and a sense of personal accomplishment that will linger long after you've returned home.

Mountain biking and e-biking

The Dolomites' dramatic peaks, pristine valleys, and endless network of scenic trails have long made this exceptional alpine region a mecca for outdoor enthusiasts. And among the most exhilarating and rewarding ways to discover the Dolomites' grandeur is through the thrill of mountain biking and e-biking.

Whether you're an experienced off-road rider or new to the sport, the Dolomites provide an unparalleled playground for two-wheeled adventure. The region's diverse terrain, which ranges from gentle, winding singletrack to challenging, technical descents, accommodates a wide range of skill levels and riding styles. And, with the growing popularity of e-bikes, even those with little cycling experience can now visit the Dolomites' most breathtaking vistas and remote trailheads.

One of the true highlights for mountain bikers and e-bikers is the Dolomiti Supertime Trail, a 130-kilometer (80-mile) network of interconnected routes that highlight the region's breathtaking natural beauty. This epic multi-day journey takes riders through a tapestry of lush meadows, ancient forests, and mountain passes, providing a fully immersive experience that highlights the Dolomites' grandeur. Along the way, a network of mountain huts, or rifugios, provide comfortable lodging and sustenance, making the Dolomiti Supertime Trail accessible to a diverse range of riders.

For those looking for a more manageable day trip, the Dolomites have a plethora of outstanding single-day rides. One such gem is the Seceda Loop, a 20-kilometer (12.4-mile) circuit that takes riders through the heart of the Puez-Odle Nature Park, offering breathtaking views of the iconic Seceda peaks and the Geisler mountain range. This moderate cross-country route is suitable for both mountain bikers and e-bikers, providing an ideal balance of challenge and scenery.

But what is the best part? You won't have to worry about packing and transporting your own bike and equipment. The Dolomites are home to a large network of bike rental outfitters, making it simple to obtain the necessary equipment upon arrival.

One highly recommended option is Dolomiti Bike, a leading provider of mountain bike and e-bike rentals with multiple locations throughout the region. Their knowledgeable staff can assist you in selecting the ideal bike for your skill level and the trails you intend to explore, with a diverse selection of models ranging from entry-level hardtails to high-performance full-suspension rigs, as well as a variety of e-bike options.

Another dependable option is Sportler, a well-known outdoor retailer with locations in many of the Dolomites' most popular destinations. In addition to bike rentals, they offer a wide range of cycling accessories, apparel, and spare parts, ensuring you have everything you need for a successful and enjoyable ride.

Many of the region's mountain huts, or rifugios, also provide on-site bike rentals, making it easy to pick up your ride at the start of your adventure and return it before settling in for the evening. This is a great option for those staying overnight in the rifugios because you won't have to worry about getting your bike to and from your accommodations.

Taking advantage of the Dolomites' extensive network of bike rental providers allows you to enjoy the freedom and exhilaration of exploring this exceptional alpine region on two wheels without having to pack and transport your own equipment. So leave your bike at home and prepare to experience the breathtaking landscapes of the Dolomites in the most thrilling way possible.

Rock climbing and via ferrata

The Dolomites are renowned not only for their breathtaking natural beauty, but also for their world-class rock climbing and via ferrata (aided climbing) routes. These vertical playgrounds offer adventurers the opportunity to push their limits and experience the region's dramatic landscapes from a truly unique perspective.

For experienced climbers, the Dolomites offer a veritable treasure trove of difficult and technically demanding crags and walls. One of the most popular destinations is the Sella Massif, a towering limestone formation with a diverse array of multi-pitch routes suitable for climbers of all skill levels. The Delago Wall, for example, is a well-known climbing destination with a number of classic routes, including the renowned Via Edelweiss, a difficult but extremely rewarding route that climbs the wall's sweeping 600-meter face.

However, the Dolomites' climbing opportunities extend far beyond the traditional rock climbing scene. The region is well-known for its extensive network of via ferrata routes, which enable both experienced and novice climbers to scale the area's sheer limestone cliffs using fixed cables, ladders, and bridges. These "iron paths" offer adventurers a thrilling and accessible way to explore the vertical landscapes of the Dolomites, all while enjoying the peace of mind that comes with the added safety features.

The Ol de Flors via ferrata, which is near the charming town of San Candido, is one of the most popular. This difficult but rewarding course takes climbers on a high-altitude journey through a dramatic limestone amphitheater with breathtaking views of the surrounding mountains and valleys. For those looking for a more family-friendly via ferrata experience, the Tre Cime di Lavaredo circuit features a well-equipped route that offers a fun and safe introduction to this unique style of mountain climbing.

Whether you choose to tackle a classic rock climbing route or embark on a via ferrata adventure, you must come prepared with the necessary gear and equipment. This includes a strong climbing harness, a certified climbing helmet, and a full via ferrata kit, which usually includes a specialized lanyard, carabiners, and shock-absorbing lanyards. To ensure your safety and enjoyment throughout your climb, you should also have the necessary skills and experience, or be accompanied by a qualified guide.

Many of the Dolomites' mountain towns and rifugios (mountain huts) provide equipment rentals as well as guided climbing and via ferrata experiences, allowing visitors to participate in these exciting activities without having to transport their own gear. Reputable outfitters, such as Edelweiss Dolomites and Vertical Adventure, offer high-quality equipment, experienced guides, and trip planning assistance to help climbers of all skill levels make the most of their Dolomites adventure.

Whether you're a seasoned rock climber or a first-time via ferratarista, the Dolomites offer an unrivaled vertical adventure that will leave you with a deep appreciation for the region's raw, breathtaking natural beauty. So lace up your climbing shoes, strap in, and prepare to conquer the Dolomites' towering limestone peaks - an experience that will undoubtedly be among your most thrilling and memorable travel experiences.

Skiing and snowboarding

When the snow blankets the Dolomites' towering peaks and valleys, the region transforms into a world-class winter sports destination that attracts skiers and snowboarders from around the globe. With its extensive network of well-groomed pistes, world-class ski resorts, and breathtaking alpine scenery, the Dolomites offer an unparalleled experience for both seasoned riders and those new to the slopes.

The Sella Ronda is a well-known 26-kilometer (16-mile) circuit that connects the resorts of Selva, Colfosco, Corvara, and Arabba. This iconic interconnected ski area offers over 500 kilometers (310 miles) of perfectly groomed runs, ranging from gentle, beginner-friendly slopes to thrilling, expert-level descents. The Sella Ronda's efficient lift system and well-marked trails make it an ideal destination for those looking to make the most of their time on the snow, while the region's mountain huts, or rifugios, provide the perfect places to refuel and take in the breathtaking scenery.

For those looking for a more immersive and off-the-beaten-path skiing or snowboarding experience, the Dolomites have a plethora of smaller, family-owned ski areas that provide a more intimate and authentic setting. One such gem is the Civetta Ski Area, which is near the charming town of Alleghe. This compact but well-equipped resort offers a mix of groomed runs and untouched powder fields, catering to a wide range of skill levels while providing a more tranquil and uncrowded alternative to larger ski areas.

Regardless of which ski area you choose to visit, the Dolomites' winter sports offerings are bolstered by the region's extensive network of ski rental and equipment shops, making it simple for visitors to get the necessary gear upon arrival. Reputable outfitters, such as Sportler and Toko, provide a diverse range of skis, snowboards, boots, and accessories, ensuring that you have everything you need for a smooth and enjoyable day on the slopes.

In addition to excellent skiing and snowboarding, the Dolomites excel at providing a comprehensive winter experience that extends beyond the slopes. Many of the region's resorts and mountain towns provide a variety of additional activities, such as scenic snowshoe hikes, cross-country skiing, ice skating, and even dog sledding, allowing visitors to fully experience the Dolomites' winter wonderland.

To fully enjoy your ski or snowboard adventure in the Dolomites, you must be prepared for the region's dynamic and often unpredictable weather conditions. Packing breathable, moisture-wicking base layers, a warm and waterproof outer shell, and appropriate winter accessories like hats, gloves, and neck warmers will help you stay comfortable and safe on the slopes.

Whether you're a seasoned shredder or a first-time snow enthusiast, the Dolomites promise an unrivaled winter sports experience that will leave you in awe of the region's natural beauty and eager to return again and again. So put on your gear, carve some turns, and prepare to discover why the Dolomites are one of the world's best winter playgrounds.

Paragliding and hang-gliding

For those seeking to experience the Dolomites' breathtaking landscapes from a truly lofty vantage point, the region's world-class paragliding and hang-gliding opportunities offer an unrivaled aerial adventure. Gliding effortlessly above towering limestone peaks, pristine alpine meadows, and crystal-clear mountain lakes, adventurers can immerse themselves in the Dolomites' grandeur like never before.

The Dolomites' unique geography and meteorological conditions make them an ideal destination for both new and experienced pilots. Thermal currents and consistent winds provide ample opportunities for long, controlled flights, while the region's diverse terrain provides a plethora of launch and landing sites to suit a wide range of skill levels and flight preferences.

Mount Kronplatz, near the charming town of Brunico, is a popular paragliding and hang-gliding destination in the Dolomites. This well-known launch site not only provides easy access to some of the region's most beautiful scenery, but it also has a well-developed infrastructure that meets the needs of both independent and tandem flyers. The nearby Dolomiti Superfly school and outfitter, for example, provides comprehensive instruction, equipment rental, and guided flights, making it an ideal choice for first-time or novice pilots seeking the thrill of airborne adventure.

For more experienced pilots, the Dolomites provide an abundance of challenging and technically demanding flying opportunities. The Sella Massif, a towering limestone formation with world-class rock climbing routes, also serves as a popular launch site for experienced paragliders and hang gliders. The area's powerful thermals and rugged, dramatic landscapes provide an ideal canvas for experienced pilots to test their limits and soar to dizzying heights.

Regardless of your level of experience, when embarking on a paragliding or hang-gliding adventure in the Dolomites, you must bring the necessary equipment and safety gear. This includes a certified, well-maintained glider, a strong harness, a protective helmet, and any emergency supplies, such as a reserve parachute and radio communication equipment.

Many of the Dolomites' paragliding and hang-gliding outfitters, such as Dolomiti Superfly and Alta Badia Flying, provide comprehensive equipment rental and training services, allowing even inexperienced flyers to take to the skies with confidence. These reputable providers also have close working relationships with local meteorological agencies, allowing them to provide up-to-date weather information and guidance to ensure the safest possible flying conditions.

For those looking for a more guided and structured experience, the Dolomites have a wealth of experienced pilots and instructors who can provide tandem flights and instruction programs tailored to a variety of skill levels. These guided experiences not only provide the necessary equipment and safety supervision, but they also give adventurers a better understanding of the art and science of free flight.

Whether you're an experienced pilot or simply looking for a new and exciting way to experience the Dolomites' unparalleled natural beauty, the region's paragliding and hang-gliding options promise an unforgettable journey through the sky. Spread your wings, take to the thermals, and soar above one of the world's most stunning alpine landscapes.

CHAPTER 5.

PLANNING YOUR DOLOMITES ADVENTURE

Best time of year to visit

The Dolomites are a true four-season destination, offering a wealth of outdoor adventures and breathtaking scenery throughout the year. However, the ideal time to visit the region can vary greatly depending on your interests, travel priorities, and tolerance for weather conditions. By carefully considering the unique advantages and considerations of each season, you can ensure that your Dolomites adventure aligns perfectly with your personal preferences and travel goals.

Spring (April - June)

As the snow melts and the alpine landscapes come to life, spring is an especially magical time to visit the Dolomites. During the shoulder season, visitors can often enjoy fewer crowds, lower lodging prices, and a tranquil, peaceful atmosphere, all while taking in the region's vibrant, emerging greenery and blooming wildflowers. This is an ideal time for hikers because many of the lower-elevation trails are clear of snow and provide stunning views of the region's iconic peaks without the intense heat of summer.

However, spring in the Dolomites can bring unpredictable weather, including sudden snowstorms and cold temperatures, particularly at higher elevations. A successful spring visit requires careful forecasting and packing appropriate, layered clothing.

Summer (July–August)

The summer months of July and August, which mark the peak of the Dolomites' tourist season, provide the most consistent weather and a diverse range of outdoor activities. During this time, the region's hiking trails, mountain biking routes, and via ferrata courses are in excellent condition, allowing adventurers to fully immerse themselves in the Dolomites' dramatic scenery. Summer's long, sunny days and mild temperatures make it an ideal time to visit the region's charming towns, sample local cuisine, and participate in vibrant cultural events and festivals.

The disadvantage of visiting the Dolomites during the summer is the possibility of crowds, higher lodging prices, and increased traffic, particularly in the region's most popular attractions. Those looking for a more peaceful and less crowded experience may want to visit during the shoulder seasons of spring or autumn instead.

Autumn (September-October)

As the summer crowds leave and the Dolomites' landscapes transform into a stunning display of autumnal colors, the fall season is a truly magical time to visit the region. During this time, hikers can enjoy the region's trails with fewer other adventurers, while mountain bikers and rock climbers can take advantage of the pleasant temperatures and conditions. The autumn also brings a sense of calm to the Dolomites' mountain towns, allowing visitors to immerse themselves in local culture and cuisine without the hustle and bustle of peak season.

However, the Dolomites' autumn weather can be unpredictable, with the possibility of unexpected snowstorms and the onset of winter conditions at higher elevations. To make the most of your Dolomites visit during this transitional season, you must plan ahead of time and have a flexible itinerary.

Winter (November to March)
For those looking for a true winter wonderland experience, the Dolomites shine during the colder months of the year. This is the peak season for snow sports enthusiasts, who can take advantage of the region's world-class ski resorts, long groomed pistes, and untracked powder fields. The Dolomites also offer a variety of other winter activities, including snowshoeing, cross-country skiing, and even dog sledding, allowing visitors to fully immerse themselves in the region's enchanting snow-covered landscapes.

The disadvantages of visiting the Dolomites in the winter include the possibility of inclement weather, road closures, and limited access to some of the region's more remote areas. A successful winter adventure in the Dolomites requires careful research, advance planning, and the willingness to be flexible.

Finally, the best time to visit the Dolomites will depend on your personal preferences, travel objectives, and weather tolerance. By taking into account the unique benefits and considerations of each season, you can tailor your Dolomites adventure to your specific needs and desires, maximizing your enjoyment and creating memories to last a lifetime.

How to get to the Dolomites

Nestled in the heart of the Italian Alps, the Dolomites are a widely accessible region that can be reached through a variety of transportation methods, each offering its own unique advantages and considerations. Whether you're traveling from within Italy, Europe, or further afield, there are several seamless options to help you plan your journey to this breathtaking alpine destination.

By Plane

For many international visitors, the most convenient way to reach the Dolomites is by flying into one of the region's closest major airports. The two primary gateways are:

Innsbruck Airport (INN) - Innsbruck Airport, located just across the border in Austria, is a popular choice, particularly for those flying from North America or other international destinations. The airport is served by a variety of airlines and provides easy access to the central Dolomites region, with numerous resorts and towns within a short drive.

Venice Marco Polo Airport (VCE) - This bustling Italian airport serves as a hub for many European and international airlines, making it an excellent choice for those arriving from within Europe. The Dolomites are approximately 2-3 hours from Venice, depending on your final destination.

To ensure a smooth journey to your Dolomites accommodations, research and compare ground transportation options such as rental cars, shuttle services, or public transportation, regardless of which airport you fly into.

By Train

For a more eco-friendly and scenic journey, the Dolomites can also be reached by train. The region's well-developed rail network, which includes high-speed and regional services, provides convenient connections from major Italian and European cities.

The Brenner Railway connects Verona (Italy) and Innsbruck (Austria), passing through the heart of the Dolomites. This journey provides breathtaking views of the region's towering peaks and lush valleys, making it an experience in and of itself.

Another excellent option is to take the train to Bolzano, a vibrant city at the foot of the Dolomites that serves as a hub for further travel throughout the region. From Bolzano, you can easily connect with local trains or buses to get to your final destination.

By Car.

Driving to the Dolomites provides the ultimate in flexibility and independence, allowing you to explore the area at your leisure and make spontaneous stops along the way. The region is well-connected by a network of scenic mountain roads and highways, allowing access from various points in Italy and neighboring countries.

If you intend to drive, it is critical to research any road conditions, closures, or restrictions, especially during the winter months when snow and ice can limit access. Consider renting a vehicle with four-wheel drive or snow tires for a safer and more comfortable journey.

Regardless of your preferred mode of transportation, it's always a good idea to plan your trip ahead of time, taking into account travel times, connections, and any reservations or bookings that may be required. Many of the Dolomites' resorts and hotels can help with transportation arrangements, so don't hesitate to contact your accommodations for advice and recommendations.

You can choose the travel option that best suits your needs and preferences by weighing factors like convenience, scenic beauty, and sustainability. This will guarantee a seamless and pleasurable trip to the stunning alpine wonderland of the Dolomites.

Entry requirements and travel documentation

As with any international destination, there are a few important entry requirements and travel documentation considerations to keep in mind when planning your Dolomites adventure. Depending on your country of origin and the duration of your stay, the specific requirements may vary, so it's essential to research and prepare well in advance to ensure a smooth and hassle-free journey.

For European Union (EU) Citizens
If you are a citizen of a European Union member state, you will not need a visa to enter Italy or the Dolomites region. All you'll need is a valid national ID card or passport. Remember that your travel document must be valid for the duration of your stay.

For non-EU citizens
Visitors from outside the European Union will typically require a Schengen visa to enter Italy and the Dolomites. The Schengen visa allows for stays of up to 90 days in the Schengen area, which includes most EU countries, as well as Switzerland, Norway, Iceland, and Liechtenstein.

To apply for a Schengen visa, submit your application and supporting documents to the Italian embassy or consulate in your home country. The application process can take several weeks, so begin the paperwork well ahead of your planned travel dates.

In addition to the Schengen visa, non-EU citizens may be required to provide proof of sufficient funds, travel health insurance, and a detailed itinerary to support their visa applications. It is critical to research the specific requirements for your nationality and the purpose of your trip, as the necessary documentation may differ.

For longer stays.
If you intend to stay in the Dolomites for more than 90 days, you will need to obtain a different type of visa, such as a student or work visa, depending on the reason for your extended stay. This process can be more complicated, so you should consult with the Italian embassy or a professional travel agent to ensure you have the necessary documentation.

To avoid delays or complications during your Dolomites adventure, make sure to prepare all necessary travel documentation ahead of time. It's always a good idea to make copies of your important documents, such as your passport, visa, and travel insurance, and store them separately from the originals.

Knowing the requirements for entry and making sure you have the required travel documents will allow you to focus on the fun of your trip to the Dolomites rather than worrying about possible bureaucratic obstacles. You'll be well on your way to enjoying the amazing adventure and beauty that this amazing alpine region has to offer with a little bit of careful planning.

Importance of travel insurance

Embarking on a journey to the Dolomites, with its awe-inspiring landscapes, thrilling outdoor activities, and charming mountain towns, is an endeavor filled with excitement and adventure. However, as with any travel experience, it's essential to protect yourself and your investment by securing comprehensive travel insurance. While the Dolomites are generally a safe and well-developed destination, the inherent risks associated with travel, combined with the region's rugged terrain and diverse range of activities, make travel insurance a crucial element of your pre-trip planning.

Coverage for Medical Emergencies
One of the primary reasons to purchase travel insurance for your Dolomites adventure is to ensure adequate coverage for any medical emergencies that may occur. The Dolomites, with their towering peaks, steep trails, and challenging outdoor activities, pose an inherent risk of injury, ranging from sprains and fractures to more serious medical conditions. If you require emergency medical care, treatment at local hospitals, or medical evacuation, your travel insurance policy can provide the financial protection and support you require, potentially saving you thousands of dollars in out-of-pocket expenses.

Many travel insurance policies provide comprehensive medical coverage, including reimbursement for doctor visits, hospital stays, and even emergency dental care. Some policies may also include provisions for medical transportation, ensuring that you receive the necessary care while being safely transported to the nearest appropriate medical facility. This coverage is especially important if you need specialized treatment or must be airlifted from a remote hiking trail or via ferrata route.

Protection for Trip Interruptions and Cancellations
In addition to medical coverage, comprehensive travel insurance can help protect your Dolomites trip in the event of unexpected interruptions or cancellations. Natural disasters, severe weather events, and even personal emergencies can all disrupt your travel plans, requiring you to change or cancel your itinerary. With the right travel insurance policy, you can be reimbursed for non-refundable pre-paid expenses like flights, accommodations, or pre-booked activities, reducing your financial losses and allowing you to reschedule or rebook your adventure at a later date.

Some policies may also cover trip delays, missed connections, or the need to shorten your trip due to a covered event, giving you the financial support you need to change your travel plans.

Coverage for Lost, Stolen, or Damaged Gear
Outdoor enthusiasts who visit the Dolomites frequently spend a significant amount of money on specialized equipment, ranging from hiking boots and climbing harnesses to ski and snowboard gear. Unfortunately, the risk of losing, stealing, or damaging these valuable items while traveling is always present. Travel insurance can cover the replacement or repair of your personal belongings, giving you peace of mind and allowing you to continue your Dolomite adventure uninterrupted.

Many travel insurance policies provide reimbursement for lost, stolen, or damaged luggage and personal items, with limits and coverage levels varying by plan. Make sure to read the fine print and understand the specific coverage details to ensure your valuable equipment is properly protected.

Choosing the Right Travel Insurance Policy.
When choosing a travel insurance policy for your Dolomites adventure, you should carefully consider your specific needs and select a plan that provides the necessary level of coverage. Consider the length of your trip, the activities you intend to participate in, any pre-existing medical conditions, and the value of your personal possessions. Additionally, look into the insurance provider's reputation and financial stability to ensure you're working with a reputable and trustworthy company.

Many travel booking websites and agencies provide integrated travel insurance options, making it easy to secure coverage at the time of trip reservation. Alternatively, you can shop around and compare policies from various independent insurance companies to find the plan that best meets your needs and budget.

Purchasing comprehensive travel insurance for your Dolomites adventure is a small cost for the peace of mind and financial security it can provide. Protecting yourself from the unexpected allows you to fully immerse yourself in the Dolomites' breathtaking landscapes, thrilling outdoor activities, and unforgettable experiences.

CHAPTER 6.

ACCOMMODATION IN THE DOLOMITES

Luxury hotels and resorts

During your venture into the captivating realm of the Dolomites, you will discover that the region's breathtaking landscapes are complemented by a stunning array of luxury hotels and resorts that offer unparalleled experiences for discerning travelers. From grand alpine chalets to contemporary architectural marvels, these prestigious properties seamlessly blend the region's natural beauty with the highest standards of hospitality and amenities.

Cristallo, a Luxury Collection Resort & Spa - Cortina d'Ampezzo

Nestled in the heart of the iconic Cortina d'Ampezzo, the Cristallo, a Luxury Collection Resort & Spa is a true gem of the Dolomites. This legendary property, known for its impeccable service and exquisite design, is situated at the base of the Tofana and Cristallo mountain ranges, offering guests breathtaking views and unparalleled access to the region's world-class skiing and hiking opportunities. The resort has 74 elegantly appointed guest rooms and suites, each with traditional Tyrolean charm complemented by modern comforts and amenities. Guests can relax in the resort's award-winning spa, enjoy gourmet cuisine at its acclaimed restaurants, and participate in a variety of on-site activities, including indoor tennis and ice skating. The Cristallo is part of the prestigious Marriott Bonvoy program, making it an excellent choice for discerning travelers looking for an unforgettable Dolomites experience. Rates begin around €500 per night, with advance booking highly recommended. For inquiries and reservations, visit www.cristallo.it or call +39 0436 3201.

Grand Hotel Dobbiaco - Toblach/Dobbiaco

Located in the picturesque town of Toblach/Dobbiaco, the Grand Hotel Dobbiaco is a stately, 5-star property that provides a luxurious retreat in the heart of the Dolomites. The hotel's prime location along the shores of Lake Dobbiaco allows for easy access to a variety of outdoor activities such as hiking, mountain biking, and cross-country skiing. The Grand Hotel Dobbiaco's 151 guest rooms and suites are tastefully furnished, with traditional alpine decor and modern amenities. Guests can enjoy the hotel's extensive wellness facilities, which include an indoor pool, sauna, and state-of-the-art fitness center. Culinary delights are served at the hotel's acclaimed restaurants, which highlight the region's exceptional local produce and wine list. Rates at the Grand Hotel Dobbiaco typically start around €350 per night, with substantial discounts available for longer stays. For more information and to book your stay, visit www.grandhoteldobbiaco.it or call +39 0474 972111.

Adler Mountain Lodge - Ortisei/St. Ulrich

Perched high above the charming village of Ortisei/St. Ulrich, the Adler Mountain Lodge provides a truly unforgettable Dolomite experience. This breathtaking, contemporary alpine retreat has 30 luxurious suites and apartments, all with panoramic views of the surrounding peaks and valleys. Guests can enjoy the lodge's exceptional wellness facilities, which include a spacious spa, an outdoor infinity pool, and a cutting-edge fitness center. The on-site restaurant serves the best regional and seasonal ingredients, while the bar and lounge provide the ideal setting for admiring the breathtaking views. With an emphasis on sustainability and environmental responsibility, the Adler Mountain Lodge is an excellent choice for discerning travelers looking for a luxurious yet environmentally conscious Dolomites adventure. Rates start at approximately €500 per night, and reservations can be made by visiting www.adler-mountain-lodge.com or calling +39 0471 775630.

Hotel Rosa Alpina - San Cassiano

Nestled in the picturesque village of San Cassiano, the Hotel Rosa Alpina is a family-owned 5-star property that has long been a favorite destination for those looking for the ultimate Dolomite experience. This grand, Tyrolean-style chalet has 52 elegantly appointed guest rooms and suites, each one reflecting the region's rich cultural heritage and breathtaking natural surroundings. Guests can relax in the hotel's world-class spa, which offers a variety of rejuvenating treatments, or sample the exceptional cuisine at the hotel's three acclaimed restaurants, including the 3-Michelin-starred St. Hubertus. The Hotel Rosa Alpina is a true gem in this alpine paradise, with impeccable service, luxurious amenities, and unparalleled access to the outdoor adventures of the Dolomites. Rates start at approximately €600 per night, and reservations can be made by visiting www.hotelrosaalpina.it or calling +39 0471 849500.

Lefay Resort & Spa Dolomiti - Pinzolo

The Lefay Resort & Spa Dolomiti, located atop the Monte Pozza in the picturesque town of Pinzolo, is a stunning, contemporary property that seamlessly combines luxury and sustainability. With 88 elegantly appointed suites, each with private terraces and panoramic mountain views, the resort provides an unparalleled wellness experience, including a 5,000 square meter spa complex, cutting-edge fitness facilities, and a holistic approach to rejuvenation. Guests can enjoy the resort's gourmet dining options, which highlight the region's exceptional local ingredients, or explore the Dolomites' world-class hiking and skiing opportunities right on the property. The Lefay Resort & Spa Dolomiti is a true oasis of calm and sophistication, making it an excellent choice for those looking for a luxurious and environmentally conscious Dolomite adventure. Rates start at approximately €550 per night, and reservations can be made by visiting www.lefayresorts.com or calling +39 0465 447000.

Schloss Seefelderhof - Seefeld

The Schloss Seefelderhof, located in the picturesque town of Seefeld, is a magnificent, historic castle that has been meticulously restored and converted into a 5-star luxury hotel. This grand 16th-century property has 46 exquisitely appointed guest rooms and suites, each of which highlights the building's original architectural elements while also providing modern comforts and amenities. Guests can enjoy the hotel's extensive wellness facilities, which include an indoor pool, saunas, and a cutting-edge fitness center, or savor the exceptional cuisine at the on-site restaurant, which celebrates the region's culinary traditions. With its proximity to the Dolomites' world-class skiing and hiking destinations, the Schloss Seefelderhof is an ideal base for those looking for a luxurious and adventurous Dolomites experience. Rates start at approximately €400 per night, and reservations can be made by visiting www.schlossseefelderhof.com or calling +43 5212 2901.

These carefully curated luxury hotels and resorts in the Dolomites provide unforgettable experiences, combining the region's breathtaking natural beauty with the highest levels of hospitality and amenities. Whether you're looking for a wellness retreat, a culinary adventure, or simply a luxurious home base for exploring the Dolomites, these properties promise to take your journey to new heights of elegance and sophistication.

Budget-friendly options

While the Dolomites are renowned for their luxurious hotels and resorts, the region also offers a wealth of more budget-friendly options that cater to a wide range of travelers. From cozy mountain inns to charming agritourism farms, these accommodations provide excellent value without compromising on the remarkable natural beauty and authentic cultural experiences that define the Dolomites.

Hotel Croce Bianca - Arabba

Nestled in the heart of the picturesque village of Arabba, the Hotel Croce Bianca is a charming, family-run establishment that provides comfortable, low-cost lodging in the Dolomites. With 40 guest rooms, the hotel offers a warm, welcoming atmosphere as well as convenient access to the region's world-class skiing and hiking opportunities. The rooms are simple but well-appointed, featuring traditional alpine decor and modern amenities. The on-site restaurant serves delicious regional cuisine, and guests can relax in the hotel's sauna and relaxation area after a day of outdoor activities. The Hotel Croce Bianca's rates typically start around €100 per night, making it an excellent choice for travelers looking for a comfortable and affordable Dolomite experience. For more information and reservations, visit www.hotelcrocebianca.com or call +39 0436 79001.

Appartamenti Residence Arnika - Canazei

The Appartamenti Residence Arnika, located in the vibrant town of Canazei, provides affordable apartment-style accommodations ideal for families and groups. The residence offers a variety of studio, one-bedroom, and two-bedroom units, all with kitchenettes, allowing guests to prepare their own meals and save money on dining out. The apartments are bright and airy, with traditional Tyrolean décor and modern amenities. Guests can also make use of the residence's sauna, game room, and outdoor terrace. The Appartamenti Residence Arnika charges around €150 per night, depending on the size and configuration of the unit. To book your stay, visit www.appartamentiresidencearnika.it or call +39 0462 601572.

Albergo Ladinia - La Villa

The Albergo Ladinia is a charming, family-run hotel in the picturesque village of La Villa that provides affordable accommodation in the heart of the Dolomites. The hotel has 26 cozy guest rooms, each with a warm and welcoming atmosphere and traditional alpine furnishings. Guests can enjoy a complimentary breakfast each morning, which includes a variety of local and homemade specialties. The Albergo Ladinia also has an on-site restaurant that serves delectable regional cuisine, as well as a wellness center with a sauna and relaxation room. Albergo Ladinia's rates typically start around €80 per night, making it an excellent choice for travelers looking for a comfortable and affordable Dolomites experience. For more information and reservations, visit www.albergoladinia.it or call +39 0471 847153.

Agriturismo Maso Stevia - Mazzin di Fassa

For travelers looking for a one-of-a-kind and affordable lodging option, Agriturismo Maso Stevia in Mazzin di Fassa is an excellent choice. This family-run agritourism farm offers cozy rooms and apartments, allowing guests to immerse themselves in the local agricultural lifestyle while also enjoying the region's exceptional food and wine. Guests can participate in farm activities like cheese-making demonstrations or explore the nearby hiking and mountain biking trails. The Agriturismo Maso Stevia's rates begin around €70 per night for double occupancy, making it an excellent value proposition for those looking for a unique and authentic Dolomite experience. Visit www.masostevia.it or call +39 0462 764228 for more information and reservations.

Hotel Garni Cesa Pianezzola - Moena

The Hotel Garni Cesa Pianezzola, located in the picturesque town of Moena, is a low-cost, family-run establishment that provides a comfortable and welcoming base for exploring the Dolomites. The hotel has 20 guest rooms, each tastefully decorated in a traditional Tyrolean style and equipped with modern amenities. Guests can begin their day with a complimentary breakfast featuring a variety of local specialties, before venturing out to enjoy the many outdoor activities available in the surrounding area. Rates at the Hotel Garni Cesa Pianezzola typically start at around €90 per night, making it an excellent choice for travelers on a budget. For reservations and more information, visit www.cesapianezzola.it or call +39 0462 573214.

Hostel Cortina - Cortina d'Ampezzo

For the best value in the Dolomites, the Hostel Cortina, located in the heart of the iconic Cortina d'Ampezzo, is an excellent choice. The hostel, which offers both dormitory-style and private rooms, provides a comfortable and sociable environment for solo travelers and groups on a tight budget. Guests can use the hostel's shared kitchen, communal lounge areas, and outdoor terrace while staying close to Cortina's world-class skiing, hiking, and cultural attractions. Rates at the Hostel Cortina start around €30 per night for a dormitory bed, making it an excellent choice for those looking for a low-cost base for their Dolomites adventure. Visit www.hostellcortina.com or call +39 0436 860391 to book your stay.

These budget-friendly accommodations in the Dolomites offer travelers the opportunity to experience the region's breathtaking natural beauty and rich cultural heritage without breaking the bank. By carefully selecting these value-driven options, you can create an unforgettable Dolomites adventure that aligns with your travel budget and preferences.

Unique stays: mountain huts and chalets

Alongside the region's luxury hotels and budget-friendly options, the Dolomites offer a remarkable collection of unique accommodations that allow travelers to fully immerse themselves in the alpine environment. From traditional mountain huts to charming Tyrolean chalets, these distinctive stays provide an unforgettable experience, blending comfort and authenticity for the ultimate Dolomites adventure.

Mountain Huts (Rifugi)

The Dolomites' rugged landscapes are dotted with a network of mountain huts known locally as "rifugi," which serve as essential resting and resupply points for hikers, climbers, and outdoor enthusiasts. These rustic yet comfortable refuges provide a unique opportunity to connect with the region's rich mountaineering heritage while also witnessing the breathtaking natural scenery up close.

One such example is the Rifugio Vajolet, which sits at an elevation of 2,243 meters in the heart of the Rosengarten massif. This traditional mountain hut offers cozy dormitory-style accommodations, a welcoming dining area serving hearty regional cuisine, and a sun terrace with panoramic views of the surrounding peaks. Rifugio Vajolet's remote location allows for easy access to a variety of hiking and climbing routes, making it a popular choice for adventurers looking for an immersive Dolomites experience. Rates usually start around €50 per person, including meals.

The Rifugio Locatelli is another well-known mountain hut, located at the foot of the iconic Tre Cime di Lavaredo (Lavaredo's Three Peaks). This historic refuge, dating back to the early twentieth century, offers both dormitory-style and private rooms to accommodate a wide range of travelers. Guests can enjoy traditional South Tyrolean cuisine, unwind in the comfortable common areas, and go on guided excursions to nearby hiking trails and climbing routes. Prices at the Rifugio Locatelli begin around €60 per person, including meals.

Tyrolean Chalets

For a more elevated and private mountain experience, the Dolomites are renowned for their charming Tyrolean chalets, which offer a cozy and luxurious home base for your alpine adventure. These traditional, wood-clad structures seamlessly blend rustic alpine charm with modern amenities, providing travelers with a truly unique and memorable stay.

The Chalet Klausnerhof, located in the picturesque village of Selva di Val Gardena, is an excellent example. This beautifully appointed chalet has six spacious suites, each with its own private balcony or terrace and stunning views of the surrounding Dolomite peaks. Guests can relax in the chalet's sauna and hot tub, eat gourmet meals prepared by the in-house chef, and take advantage of the numerous hiking and skiing opportunities nearby. Rates at the Chalet Klausnerhof typically begin around €300 per night, with discounts available for longer stays.

Another stunning Tyrolean chalet option is the Chalet Zallinger, located in the picturesque village of Alpe di Siusi. This luxurious 8-suite property has a refined, contemporary design that pays homage to the area's traditional architectural style. Guests can unwind in the chalet's indoor pool, indulge in a spa treatment, and savor exceptional cuisine at the on-site restaurant, all while admiring the breathtaking views of the surrounding Dolomite mountains. Rates at the Chalet Zallinger begin around €450 per night, making it an indulgent yet unforgettable Dolomites experience.

Whether you stay in a cozy mountain hut or a charming Tyrolean chalet, these unique accommodations allow visitors to fully immerse themselves in the Dolomites' breathtaking natural setting and rich cultural heritage. By choosing these unique accommodations, you can create an adventure that goes beyond the typical hotel experience, allowing you to form a stronger bond with the region's rugged beauty and adventurous spirit.

Tips for booking accommodations

Securing the perfect accommodations is a crucial element of planning your Dolomites adventure. With a diverse range of options, from luxurious resorts to cozy mountain huts, navigating the booking process can be daunting. To ensure a seamless experience, consider the following tips:

Plan Ahead: The Dolomites are a popular tourist destination, particularly during peak summer and winter seasons. To secure your preferred accommodations, book well in advance, typically 6-12 months before your travel dates. This is especially important for in-demand properties and one-of-a-kind stays, like mountain huts and exclusive chalets.

Consider Shoulder Seasons: If your travel dates are flexible, consider visiting the Dolomites in the spring or fall. These times have more availability and frequently lower rates, while still allowing access to the region's stunning natural beauty and a variety of outdoor activities.

Research Reputable Booking Platforms: When booking your Dolomites accommodations, use reputable platforms such as official tourism websites (www.dolomiti.org), hotel booking sites (Booking.com, Expedia, etc.), or the property's website. This ensures that you are dealing with legitimate companies and can take advantage of any special offers or package deals.

Understand Cancellation Policies: Carefully review your chosen accommodations' cancellation and modification policies. Many properties in the Dolomites have strict policies, especially during peak seasons, so make sure you understand the terms to avoid any unexpected fees or penalties.

Consider Package Deals: Look for packages that combine lodging with other services, such as lift passes, equipment rentals, or guided activities. These packages can often offer significant cost savings and convenience, particularly for first-time visitors to the Dolomites.

Communicate Preferences: When booking your accommodations, include any special requests or needs, such as room configurations, accessibility requirements, or dietary restrictions. Many properties in the Dolomites are eager to accommodate their guests and will go above and beyond to make their stay as comfortable and enjoyable as possible.

Consider Alternative Accommodations: In addition to traditional hotels and resorts, look into vacation rentals, agritourism farms, and mountain huts. These unique options can provide a more immersive and cost-effective Dolomite experience.

Seek Local Expertise: Ask local tourism boards, hiking associations, or outdoor activity providers for recommendations on the best accommodations for your specific activities and interests. Their insider knowledge can be extremely useful in determining the best fit for your Dolomites adventure.

Following these tips and utilizing the wealth of resources available will allow you to confidently navigate the Dolomites' accommodation landscape, ensuring a seamless and unforgettable experience in this breathtaking alpine region.

CHAPTER 7.

CULTURAL EXPERIENCES IN THE DOLOMITES

Traditional festivals and events

The Dolomites region is renowned not only for its breathtaking natural beauty but also for its rich cultural heritage, which is celebrated through a vibrant calendar of traditional festivals and events. From centuries-old religious celebrations to lively, community-driven festivities, these cultural experiences offer visitors a unique glimpse into the heart and soul of the Dolomites.

Südtiroler Almabtrieb (South Tyrolean Cattle Drive) - September/October

The Südtiroler Almabtrieb, or South Tyrolean Cattle Drive, is one of the Dolomites' most iconic cultural events, taking place every fall. This centuries-old tradition commemorates the cattle's return from summer pastures in the high alpine meadows to their winter quarters in the valley. Visitors are encouraged to watch the procession of elaborately decorated cows, adorned with colorful ribbons and flowers, as they are led down from the mountain pastures by local farmers and families. The Almabtrieb is celebrated in many towns and villages throughout the Dolomites, but we recommend spending it in the charming town of Kastelruth/Castelrotto, where the event is especially lively and well-attended. Immerse yourself in the festive atmosphere, enjoy traditional music and dance performances, and savor the region's delectable cuisine to truly embrace the Dolomites' cultural heritage.

Ladin Cultural Festival – July

The Ladin Cultural Festival, which takes place every July in the Dolomites' Val Badia region, is a must-see event for anyone interested in Ladin culture and languages. The Ladins are an indigenous ethnic group whose language and traditions have been influenced by the region's harsh alpine environment. The festival commemorates this rich cultural heritage with a lively program of music, dance, traditional crafts, and culinary demonstrations. Attend the festival in the picturesque town of Badia/La Valle to see traditional costume parades, participate in Ladin language workshops, and sample the region's authentic cuisine. This event offers a unique opportunity to gain a better understanding and appreciation for the Dolomites' cultural diversity.

Törggelen - October/November

As the leaves turn golden and the air becomes crisp in the Dolomites, the Törggelen festival kicks off the autumn season with a celebration of regional food and wine. Törggelen is a time-honored tradition that began in South Tyrol, where local farmers and vintners invite visitors to their "Stube" (parlors) to sample the year's new wine, which is accompanied by a spread of traditional dishes such as roasted chestnuts, "Kiachl" (fried pastries), and hearty South Tyrolean fare. We recommend attending the Törggelen celebrations in the charming town of Merano, where you can stroll through the cozy village streets, visit historic wine cellars, and soak up the convivial atmosphere that defines this autumnal festival.

Krampus Run - Early December

Plan your trip to the Dolomites around the Krampus Run, a centuries-old tradition held in early December. This event celebrates the Krampus, a horned, demonic figure from Alpine folklore, with locals donning elaborate, handcrafted costumes and masks and marching through the streets in boisterous parades. Witness the Krampus figures roaming the town centers, accompanied by cowbells ringing and whips cracking, creating a surreal and captivating display of traditional Tyrolean culture. One of the best places to see the Krampus Run is in Brixen/Bressanone, where the event is exceptionally well-organized and attracts large crowds of both locals and curious visitors.

Dolomiti Ski Jazz Festival - March

For music lovers visiting the Dolomites, the Dolomiti Ski Jazz Festival is a must-see event. This unique festival, held every March, combines the region's world-class skiing with the vibrant sounds of live jazz performances. A diverse lineup of jazz artists, from renowned international musicians to local talents, performs in venues throughout Cortina d'Ampezzo, Misurina, and Toblach/Dobbiaco ski resorts. Spend your days on the slopes, then immerse yourself in the festival's vibrant atmosphere, enjoying the unique blend of winter sports and jazz culture that distinguishes this event. The Dolomiti Ski Jazz Festival is a true celebration of the Dolomites' multifaceted appeal, combining outdoor adventure with artistic expression.

These traditional festivals and events provide visitors to the Dolomites with the opportunity to immerse themselves in the region's rich cultural heritage, witnessing customs, cuisines, and celebrations passed down through generations. Whether you're drawn to the Almabtrieb's festive pageantry, the captivating Ladin cultural traditions, or the unique combination of winter sports and jazz, these events promise to enrich your Dolomites adventure with unforgettable cultural immersion.

Local cuisine and culinary highlights

The Dolomites region is renowned not only for its breathtaking natural beauty but also for its exceptional and diverse culinary traditions. Blending the influences of Italian, Austrian, and Ladin cultures, the local cuisine of the Dolomites offers a unique and delectable gastronomic experience for visitors.

South Tyrolean Specialties

South Tyrol's traditional dishes, which have strong cultural ties to both Italy and Austria, are central to the Dolomites' culinary identity. One of the most famous South Tyrolean specialties is "Speck," which is cured and smoked pork that is commonly served as an appetizer or used as an ingredient in a variety of regional dishes. Another must-try is "Schlutzkrapfen," a ravioli filled with ricotta, spinach, or potatoes and topped with melted butter and grated cheese. For a heartier option, try the "Canederli," South Tyrolean bread dumplings that are frequently served in broth or with roasted meat. These traditional dishes can be found in charming local restaurants and farmhouses throughout the Dolomites, giving visitors a true taste of the region's culinary heritage.

Ladin Cuisine

The Ladin people, an indigenous ethnic group of the Dolomites, have also had a significant impact on the region's culinary landscape. Ladin cuisine is distinguished by its use of locally sourced ingredients such as mountain herbs, dairy products, and game meat. One traditional Ladin dish is "Pizzoccheri," a short, wide buckwheat noodle served with potatoes, cabbage, and a rich cheese sauce. Another Ladin specialty is "Strangolapreti," or "priest stranglers," a type of gnocchi made from bread, spinach, and cheese that is frequently served with a sage-flavored butter sauce. When visiting the Ladin-speaking valleys of the Dolomites, such as Val Badia and Val di Fassa, make sure to try these traditional Ladin culinary delights.

Foraged and Seasonal Ingredients

The Dolomites' rugged alpine landscape produces a bounty of wild, foraged ingredients, which are celebrated in the region's cuisine. Local chefs and home cooks use everything from mountain herbs and wild mushrooms to berries and edible flowers in their dishes, highlighting the Dolomites' abundant natural resources. In the spring, "Ramsons," or wild garlic, may appear in pastas, soups, and sauces, while the summer brings an abundance of wild berries and alpine strawberries. Autumn brings prized porcini mushrooms and the sweet, nutty chestnuts that are central to the Törggelen festival. By embracing seasonal, locally sourced ingredients, the Dolomites' culinary scene reflects the natural world's rhythm and the deep connection between land and table.

Dairy and Cheese

The rolling alpine meadows and lush pastures of the Dolomites create ideal conditions for dairy farming, resulting in a rich cheesemaking tradition in the region. The Dolomites are a cheese lover's paradise, with creamy, soft "Malga" cheeses made by mountain herders and firm, aged "Asiago" and "Montasio" varieties. Visitors are encouraged to visit local creameries, dairy farms, and mountain huts to observe the cheesemaking process and sample the region's famous dairy products. Don't pass up the opportunity to try a classic "Canederli" dish, which features these delectable cheeses as the star.

Wine & Grappa

In addition to the Dolomites' exceptional culinary offerings, the region has a thriving winemaking tradition, particularly in South Tyrol's sunny, south-facing valleys. The Dolomites' crisp, aromatic white wines, such as Gewürztraminer and Müller-Thurgau, are known for their superior quality and distinct alpine character. In addition, the region produces exceptional red wines such as the robust Lagrein and the lighter, more delicate Schiava. For a true taste of local spirit, try the region's signature grappa, a potent distilled beverage made from local grape pomace. Whether you're sipping a glass of Dolomites wine or enjoying a smooth grappa, you'll be immersed in the region's rich viticultural history.

From traditional South Tyrolean dishes to foraged, seasonal delights, as well as exceptional dairy and wine offerings, the Dolomites' culinary landscape is a sensory feast. Visitors who indulge in these local specialties can gain a better understanding and appreciation for the region's cultural identity, as well as the strong bond between the land, the people, and the food that sustains them.

Museums and heritage sites

The Dolomites region is a true cultural tapestry, with a rich history and heritage that is celebrated and preserved through an impressive array of museums and heritage sites. From immersive alpine ethnographic displays to world-class art collections, these institutions offer visitors a window into the diverse cultural influences that have shaped the Dolomites over the centuries.

Messner Mountain Museum (MMM) - Locations Across the Dolomites

The Messner Mountain Museum (MMM), a network of six interconnected museum locations designed by renowned mountaineer Reinhold Messner, stands out in the Dolomites' cultural landscape. Each MMM site focuses on a different aspect of mountain culture, such as the history of alpinism or the relationship between humans and the alpine environment.

The MMM Corones, located atop the Kronplatz mountain in South Tyrol, is a particular highlight, providing visitors with an unparalleled, immersive experience of mountain life. Designed by renowned architect Zaha Hadid, the museum's striking, contemporary architecture blends seamlessly with the surrounding Dolomite peaks, inviting visitors to explore exhibits that delve into the physical and psychological challenges of mountain climbing.

Another must-see MMM location is the MMM Firmian, located in the historic Castel Firmiano near Bolzano. This museum documents the evolution of alpinism, from early pioneers to modern adventurers, and features an impressive collection of mountaineering artifacts and equipment. The MMM Firmian's strategic location at the foot of the Dolomites provides an ideal setting for contextualizing the region's rich mountaineering heritage.

Ladin Museum (Museo Ladin) – Val Badia

A visit to the Ladin Museum in the town of San Martino in Badia/St. Martin in Thurn is a must for those interested in learning more about the culture. The Ladin people are an indigenous ethnic group whose language and traditions have been shaped by the Dolomites' rugged alpine environment, and this museum provides a comprehensive look at their distinct heritage.

Interactive exhibits and multimedia displays allow visitors to learn the Ladin language, traditional crafts and costumes, and the region's agricultural and pastoral history. The museum's carefully curated collection of Ladin artifacts, which includes intricately decorated ceramics, textiles, and folk art, gives visitors a real sense of the resilient mountain community's daily lives and customs.

By visiting the Ladin Museum, visitors gain a better understanding of the cultural diversity that thrives in the Dolomites, and the museum's knowledgeable staff is eager to share their insights and facilitate a truly immersive experience.

Museo Ladino di Fassa - Vigo di Fassa

In addition to the Ladin Museum in Val Badia, the Museo Ladino di Fassa, located in the picturesque town of Vigo di Fassa. This museum provides a comprehensive exploration of Fassa Valley-specific Ladin culture, language, and traditions, giving visitors a unique opportunity to witness the nuances and variations that exist within the broader Ladin identity.

The Museo Ladino di Fassa's highlights include an extensive collection of traditional Ladin costumes, intricate woodcarvings, and historical agricultural implements, all displayed in beautifully curated exhibitions. The museum also has interactive elements, such as language workshops and demonstrations of traditional crafts, which allow visitors to actively participate in and learn about the Ladin way of life.

One of the museum's most appealing aspects is its dedication to preserving and promoting the Ladin language, which is classified as a minority language in the Dolomites. Visitors to the Museo Ladino di Fassa gain a better understanding of the Ladin people's ongoing efforts to preserve their linguistic and cultural heritage in the face of modernization and external influences.

Dolomiti Bellunesi National Park Visitor Center, Feltre
For those interested in the Dolomites' rich natural heritage, a visit to the Dolomiti Bellunesi National Park Visitor Center in Feltre is strongly recommended. This cutting-edge facility serves as the park's entrance, providing visitors with an in-depth look at the region's unique geology, flora, and fauna.

The interactive exhibits and multimedia displays at the Visitor Center explain how the Dolomite mountains formed, how plants and animals adapt to the alpine environment, and how important it is to preserve this UNESCO World Heritage site. Visitors can also learn about the park's hiking trails and outdoor activities, ensuring that they are well-prepared to fully enjoy the natural wonders of the Dolomites.

What distinguishes the Dolomiti Bellunesi National Park Visitor Center is its dedication to environmental education and sustainability. The facility itself is an example of environmentally friendly design, incorporating renewable energy sources and sustainable construction materials, emphasizing the Dolomites' role as a natural conservation hotspot.

Mercantia-Certaldo, Tuscany
While not located in the Dolomites, the Mercantia festival in Certaldo, Tuscany, is a cultural event with strong ties to the alpine region. Mercantia, which takes place every July, is a vibrant celebration of street performance, medieval reenactments, and traditional craftsmanship inspired by the Dolomites' and the Italian Alps' rich cultural heritage.

Visitors to Mercantia can expect to be captivated by the festival's enchanting atmosphere, as the historic town of Certaldo is transformed into a living, breathing outdoor museum. Wander through the winding streets and alleyways to see acrobatic performances, puppet shows, and the creation of handcrafted artisanal goods, all while immersing yourself in the spirit of the Dolomites' cultural heritage.

While not a direct Dolomites experience, the Mercantia festival provides a complementary cultural exploration, allowing visitors to draw connections between the Dolomites and the rest of Italy's alpine region, fostering a deeper appreciation for the diverse tapestry of traditions and influences that have shaped this remarkable landscape.

These museums and heritage sites, located throughout the Dolomites and beyond, provide visitors with an unparalleled opportunity to learn about the region's rich cultural history and the diverse influences that have shaped its distinct identity. Whether you're drawn to the breathtaking mountain landscapes, the resilient Ladin people, or the enduring legacy of alpinism, these institutions offer a multifaceted lens through which to understand and appreciate the Dolomites' cultural significance.

Artisan crafts and workshops

Alongside the Dolomites' breathtaking natural landscapes and cultural heritage, the region is also renowned for its vibrant artisanal traditions, which have been passed down through generations. From intricate woodcarvings to handwoven textiles, the Dolomites are home to a thriving community of skilled craftspeople who continue to honor and preserve these time-honored techniques.

Woodcarving

Woodcarving is one of the Dolomites' most iconic artisanal crafts. The region's dense forests and abundant timber resources have long provided materials for local artisans to create a diverse range of exquisite wooden objects, from intricately detailed religious figurines to functional household goods.

In the charming town of Ortisei/St. Ulrich, visitors can immerse themselves in the woodcarving tradition by visiting local artisans' workshops. You can watch the meticulous process of transforming raw wood into intricate, lifelike sculptures, which frequently depict the region's alpine fauna or religious icons. Many of these workshops also provide demonstrations and hands-on workshops, allowing visitors to try their hand at this time-honored craft while guided by skilled artisans.

Selva di Val Gardena, another well-known woodcarving center in the Dolomites, has seen generations of families hone their skills in this artistic discipline. Visitors can wander through the various workshops and galleries, admiring the exquisite craftsmanship and possibly commissioning a custom piece to take home as a unique memento of their Dolomites adventure.

Ladin Textile and Embroidery

The Ladins of the Dolomites have long been known for their exceptional textile arts, particularly the intricate embroidery and weaving techniques that have become an integral part of their cultural heritage. These traditional textiles, which frequently feature geometric patterns and vibrant colors inspired by the alpine landscape, can be found in traditional costumes, household linens, and decorative accessories.

Visitors to the Dolomites' Ladin-speaking valleys, such as Val Badia and Val di Fassa, can immerse themselves in the rich textile heritage by visiting local workshops and studios. Here, skilled artisans demonstrate the laborious process of hand-weaving fabrics on traditional looms, as well as the delicate art of embroidering intricate patterns with time-honored stitching techniques.

These workshops not only teach about the Ladin textile tradition, but also allow participants to purchase one-of-a-kind, handcrafted items to take home. These artisanal textiles, ranging from vibrant woven blankets to delicately embroidered cushions, serve as tangible reminders of the Dolomites' cultural vibrancy and the people's enduring creativity.

Ceramics and Pottery

The Dolomites' abundant natural resources have also fueled a thriving tradition of ceramic and pottery production, with local artisans producing a wide range of functional and decorative items. The Dolomites are home to a diverse range of ceramic styles and techniques, from the iconic "Maiolica" glazed pottery of the Valsugana region to the intricate, hand-painted ceramics of the Ladin valleys.

The Ceramica Decorata in Canazei is a must-see ceramic workshop, where master potter Giancarlo Rizzi and his family have been producing exquisite, hand-painted ceramic pieces for generations. Visitors can watch as skilled artisans transform raw clay into beautifully decorated plates, bowls, and other everyday items, infusing them with vibrant colors and patterns inspired by the surrounding Dolomite landscape.

In addition to purchasing these one-of-a-kind ceramic creations, many workshops provide hands-on pottery-making classes, allowing visitors to try their hand at the potter's wheel and gain a better understanding of the skill and artistry involved in this ancient craft.

Metalwork and Jewelry

The Dolomites' artisanal traditions go beyond textiles and ceramics, with a strong heritage in metalworking and jewelry making. Local artisans have long used the region's mineral resources to create a wide range of exquisite metal objects, including intricate religious artifacts and delicate, handcrafted jewelry.

Visitors can visit the workshop of master silversmith Claudio Gisonda in Campione d'Italia, which is just across the border from Italy's Dolomites. Gisonda and his team of skilled artisans create stunning, custom-made silver jewelry inspired by the rugged alpine environment, featuring motifs of mountain peaks, wildflowers, and local wildlife.

Similarly, in the Ladin-speaking valley of Val di Fassa, the town of Moena has a long history of metalworking, with local artisans creating one-of-a-kind items like decorative wrought-iron pieces and traditional Ladin-style jewelry. Visitors can explore these workshops, see the meticulous techniques used, and even commission custom pieces to commemorate their Dolomites adventure.

Visitors can learn more about the rich cultural legacy of the Dolomites and the talented individuals who uphold these age-old customs by spending time in the artisanal workshops and studios.

Whether you are admiring beautiful metalwork, delicate textiles, or intricate woodcarvings, these encounters with local artisans offer a memorable and authentic connection to the Dolomites' ever-present creative spirit.

CHAPTER 8.

NATURE AND WILDLIFE IN THE DOLOMITES

National parks and nature reserves

The Dolomites region is a true natural wonder, boasting a diverse and awe-inspiring landscape that has been meticulously preserved through a network of national parks and nature reserves. These protected areas offer visitors an unparalleled opportunity to immerse themselves in the region's breathtaking geology, diverse ecosystems, and abundant wildlife. Whether you're an avid hiker, a wildlife enthusiast, or simply someone seeking to connect with the great outdoors, these Dolomites natural sanctuaries are sure to leave a lasting impression.

Parco Naturale Dolomiti Bellunesi (Dolomiti Bellunesi National Park)

The Parco Naturale Dolomiti Bellunesi, located in the heart of the Dolomites, is the region's true gem, encompassing over 31,000 hectares of pristine alpine landscapes. This national park, a UNESCO World Heritage site, is well-known for its dramatic, jagged peaks, serene valleys, and diverse flora and fauna.

One of the park's main attractions is the iconic Pale di San Martino massif, a towering limestone formation that exemplifies the Dolomites' geological wonders. Visitors can explore this natural spectacle via a network of well-marked hiking trails, which provide breathtaking views and opportunities to spot the park's resident wildlife, including chamois, ibex, and the elusive Eurasian lynx.

In addition to its breathtaking scenery, the Parco Naturale Dolomiti Bellunesi boasts a rich cultural heritage, including historic villages, traditional mountain huts, and artisanal workshops that provide a deeper connection to the region's past. We recommend spending at least a few days immersed in this national park, allowing plenty of time to discover its hidden gems and truly appreciate the Dolomites' majesty.

Adamello Brenta Nature Park

The Parco Naturale Adamello Brenta, which spans the border between Trentino and Lombardy, is a nature lover's dream, covering nearly 62,000 hectares of pristine alpine landscapes. This expansive park is known for its dramatic glaciers, crystalline lakes, and diverse wildlife, making it an ideal destination for outdoor enthusiasts.

One of the park's most captivating features is the Adamello Glacier, the largest glacier in the Italian Alps. Visitors can take guided tours to explore the intricate network of ice caves and seracs that cover the glacier's surface, providing a unique perspective on the region's glacial formations. For a more panoramic view, take the Adamello Ski Area cable car to the summit of Monte Spinale, where you can admire the park's breathtaking views.

In addition to its glacial wonders, the Parco Naturale Adamello Brenta supports a diverse range of flora and fauna, including the iconic brown bear. While sightings of this elusive creature are uncommon, the park's well-marked hiking trails and wildlife observation areas offer the best chances of seeing this majestic predator, as well as other alpine species like ibex and golden eagles.

When visiting the Parco Naturale Adamello Brenta, make time to explore the park's traditional mountain villages, which provide insight into the region's cultural heritage and the long-standing relationship between local communities and the natural environment.

Parco Naturale Fanes-Senes-Braies (Fanes-Sennes-Braies Nature Park)

The Parco Naturale Fanes-Senes-Braies, located in the northeastern corner of the Dolomites, is a true gem of the region, providing visitors with a breathtaking tapestry of alpine landscapes and diverse ecosystems. This nature park, which covers over 25,000 hectares, is known for its stunning rock formations, pristine lakes, and abundance of wildlife.

Braies Lake, a stunning, turquoise-hued body of water surrounded by the dramatic Croda del Becco and Seekofel mountains, is one of the park's most captivating features. Visitors can explore the lake's shores on foot or by boat, admiring the stunning reflections of the surrounding peaks and the diverse birdlife that inhabits the area.

For those looking for a more challenging adventure, the Parco Naturale Fanes-Senes-Braies has a vast network of hiking trails that wind through the park's diverse landscapes, ranging from lush alpine meadows to rugged mountain passes. Hikers may see the park's resident wildlife, such as the nimble chamois, the elusive lynx, and the majestic golden eagle.

In addition to its natural wonders, the Parco Naturale Fanes-Senes-Braies has an extensive cultural heritage, including historic mountain huts and traditional Ladin villages that offer a glimpse into the region's past. We strongly advise taking at least a few days to fully explore this captivating nature park, immersing yourself in the Dolomites' breathtaking landscapes and the enduring relationship between the land and its people.

Parco Naturale Paneveggio-Pale di San Martino (Paneveggio-Pale di San Martino Nature Park)

The Parco Naturale Paneveggio-Pale di San Martino, located in the southern reaches of the Dolomites, is a true natural wonder, spanning over 19,000 hectares of pristine alpine landscapes. This park is well-known for its diverse ecosystems, which range from ancient spruce forests to stunning glacial lakes and serve as a haven for a variety of wildlife species.

The Pale di San Martino massif, a towering limestone formation that rises majestically from the surrounding landscape, is one of the park's most identifiable features. Visitors can explore a variety of hiking trails that provide breathtaking views of this natural wonder, as well as opportunities to see the park's resident wildlife, such as the majestic golden eagle and the elusive Eurasian Lynx.

For those looking for a more immersive experience, the Parco Naturale Paneveggio-Pale di San Martino provides a network of well-equipped mountain huts and refuges, allowing visitors to fully immerse themselves in the park's tranquil surroundings and gain a deeper appreciation for the Dolomites' natural heritage. Keep an eye out for the park's famous "Resonance Spruce" trees, which have been used for centuries to make the well-known violins of nearby Cremona.

Whether you're drawn to the park's breathtaking scenery, diverse wildlife, or rich cultural heritage, the Parco Naturale Paneveggio-Pale di San Martino is a must-see destination for anyone looking to connect with the natural wonders of the Dolomites.

These national parks and nature reserves are the pinnacles of the Dolomites' natural heritage, displaying the region's breathtaking geology, diverse ecosystems, and abundant wildlife. Exploring these protected areas allows visitors to not only immerse themselves in the breathtaking landscapes of the Dolomites, but also gain a better understanding of the ongoing efforts to preserve this UNESCO World Heritage site for future generations. We strongly advise allotting enough time to fully appreciate the natural wonders of the Dolomites, allowing yourself to be captivated by the raw power and timeless beauty of this remarkable alpine region.

Flora and fauna of the region

The Dolomites region is a true natural treasure trove, boasting a remarkable diversity of plant and animal life that has adapted to the rugged alpine environment over millennia. From the vibrant wildflowers that dot the region's meadows to the elusive predators that roam its peaks, the Dolomites' flora and fauna are a testament to the resilience and adaptability of life in this remarkable mountain landscape.

Flora of the Dolomites

The Dolomites' diverse geological formations and microclimates have resulted in a rich tapestry of plant life, with over 2,000 species of vascular plants living here. As you explore the national parks and nature reserves, you'll be greeted by a spectacular display of wildflowers that bloom during the warmer months, transforming the landscape into a vibrant patchwork of color.

One of the Dolomites' most famous floral displays is the explosion of alpine meadows that appear in the valleys and along the mountain slopes. These meadows are a kaleidoscope of colors, with species like bright-yellow arnica, delicate edelweiss, and vibrant red campion flourishing in the well-drained, nutrient-rich soil. Many of these plants have developed unique strategies to survive the Dolomites' harsh winters, such as deep, extensive root systems and protective leaf structures.

Beyond the meadows, the Dolomites are home to a diverse range of coniferous and deciduous tree species, such as the towering European larch, the hardy mountain pine, and the stately Swiss stone pine. These hardy trees not only provide critical habitat for the region's wildlife, but they also help to stabilize the slopes and prevent erosion.

The "Resonance Spruces" found in Parco Naturale Paneveggio-Pale di San Martino are especially noteworthy. These ancient spruce trees, with their distinctive straight, fine-grained trunks, have long been prized by violin makers in Cremona for their exceptional resonant properties.

Fauna of the Dolomites
The Dolomites' diverse ecosystems support a diverse range of wildlife, from graceful chamois navigating steep, rocky terrain to elusive predators prowling high-altitude forests and meadows.

The majestic brown bear, one of the Dolomites' most celebrated residents, has made a remarkable comeback in recent decades as a result of conservation efforts. While spotting these elusive creatures in the wild can be difficult, the Parco Naturale Adamello Brenta provides the best opportunities, with designated wildlife observation areas and well-marked hiking trails that lead through the bears' natural habitat.

The Dolomites also have large ungulate populations, including the nimble-footed chamois and the imposing Eurasian ibex. These hardy, sure-footed creatures can be seen grazing in the alpine meadows or negotiating the region's steep, rocky slopes with remarkable agility. Keen-eyed visitors may also catch a glimpse of the elusive Eurasian lynx, a rare and enigmatic predator that is slowly making a comeback in the Dolomites.

The Dolomites have a diverse avian fauna, including the majestic golden eagle, the graceful peregrine falcon, and the vibrant rock partridge. Birdwatchers will enjoy the opportunity to see these magnificent creatures soaring through the mountain air or foraging among the alpine vegetation.

Beyond the region's larger, more charismatic species, the Dolomites are home to a diverse range of smaller mammals, reptiles, amphibians, and invertebrates, all of which play important roles in the delicate balance of alpine ecosystems. From the agile rock ptarmigan to the hardworking marmot, these creatures are an essential part of the Dolomites' natural tapestry, contributing to the region's long-term ecological richness.

As you explore the Dolomites, keep your eyes open and your senses alert to the abundance of life that thrives in this breathtaking mountain landscape. Whether you're admiring the vibrant wildflowers, tracking the movements of a majestic ibex, or simply listening to the calls of the local birds, you'll be captivated by the natural wonders that make the Dolomites such a unique and valuable treasure.

Scenic drives and viewpoints

The Dolomites, with their dramatic limestone peaks, lush alpine meadows, and winding valleys, offer some of the most breathtaking scenic drives and viewpoints in all of Europe. As you navigate the region's well-maintained roads and hiking trails, you'll be treated to a stunning panorama of natural wonders that will leave a lasting impression. Whether you're seeking panoramic vistas, picturesque villages, or opportunities to connect with the great outdoors, the Dolomites' scenic routes and viewpoints are sure to captivate and inspire.

The Great Dolomites Road (Großglockner Hochalpenstraße)
The 48-kilometer Großglockner Hochalpenstraße, also known as the Great Dolomites Road, is a renowned scenic drive in the Dolomites that provides an incredibly breathtaking experience. This route offers you a front-row seat to the natural grandeur of the Dolomites as it winds through the Hohe Tauern National Park, passing through a dramatic landscape of towering peaks, lush alpine meadows, and cascading waterfalls.

The Great Dolomites Road has a lot of beautiful viewpoints, hiking trails, and charming mountain villages that are worth exploring, so we strongly advise planning to spend at least a full day exploring it. Make sure to stop at the historic mountain hut known as the Blaueishütte, where you can enjoy traditional Tyrolean cuisine and breathtaking views of the surrounding peaks.

We recommend scheduling your visit for the summer, when the weather is mild and the roads are free of snow, for the best possible experience. But bear in mind that during the busiest travel season, this well-traveled route can get very crowded, so if you want to avoid the crowds, try going early in the day or visiting on a weekday.

The Dolomites Panoramic Road (Dolomites Höhenstraße)
The Dolomites Panoramic Road, also known as Dolomites Höhenstraße, is a 100-kilometer route that winds through the center of the Parco Naturale Fanes-Sennes-Braies. It is another well-known scenic drive in the Dolomites. With a plethora of

pullouts and viewpoints that let you fully immerse yourself in the natural beauty, this breathtaking road offers a unique perspective on the region's stunning limestone formations.

The tranquil, turquoise-hued Lago di Braies is a must-see location along the Dolomites Panoramic Road. It is encircled by the striking peaks of the Croda del Becco and Seekofel mountains. We suggest dedicating a minimum of several hours to stroll along the lake's shoreline or rent a classic wooden boat, and relish in the breathtaking views of the reflected peaks.

The Passo Valparola, a picturesque mountain pass that provides breath-taking views of the Fanes-Sennes-Braies Nature Park, is another highlight of the Dolomites Panoramic Road. You can hike along clearly marked trails here to see alpine flora and fauna, or you can just unwind and enjoy the expansive views.

We recommend scheduling your visit during the shoulder seasons of spring and fall, when there are fewer crowds and the weather is typically mild and clear, to fully enjoy the Dolomites Panoramic

Road. Make sure you are conversant with the driving laws of the area as well, since certain roads may have limitations or tolls.

The Cortina d'Ampezzo Scenic Drive

The Cortina d'Ampezzo Scenic Drive, which winds through the quaint town of Cortina d'Ampezzo and the surrounding Ampezzo Valley, provides a delightful alternative for those looking for a more intimate, local experience. This charming route passes by old churches, homes built in the traditional Ladin style, and breathtaking views of the Cristallo and Tofane mountain ranges.

The opportunity to visit the Museo dell'Orologeria, a fascinating museum devoted to the craft of clock and watchmaking, is one of the highlights of the Cortina d'Ampezzo Scenic Drive. Here, you can see expert craftspeople in action and discover more about the area's rich history in watchmaking.

The Santuario di Nostra Signora delle Grazie, a breathtaking Baroque-style church that provides a tranquil escape from the bustle of the town, is another must-see location along this route. Take some time to appreciate the church's elaborate altarpieces and frescoes, which offer insights into the deeply held religious traditions of the area.

We suggest visiting Cortina d'Ampezzo in the summertime, when the town is bustling with outdoor festivals, cultural activities, and chances to explore the surrounding natural beauty on foot or by bicycle, for the best possible experience. Remember that this is a popular area, so during the busiest travel season, expect slightly higher prices and more people.

The Alta Via 1 Hiking Trail
While not a traditional scenic drive, the Alta Via 1 hiking trail is a must-mention for those seeking a truly immersive Dolomites experience. Spanning over 120 kilometers, this renowned long-distance trail offers some of the most breathtaking vistas in the entire region, with panoramic views of jagged limestone peaks, serene alpine lakes, and lush meadows.

The Alta Via 1 is not for the faint of heart, as it involves several days of challenging hiking through rugged terrain. However, the rewards are well worth the effort, as you'll have the opportunity to stay in historic mountain huts, witness the region's diverse flora and fauna, and reconnect with the natural world in a truly profound way.

If you're considering tackling the Alta Via 1, we recommend allotting at least 7-10 days to complete the full trail, and ensuring that you're well-prepared with proper hiking gear, navigation skills, and a good level of physical fitness. Be sure to also research the trail conditions and weather forecasts, as the Dolomites can experience sudden and dramatic changes in weather.

Whether you opt for a leisurely scenic drive or a more challenging hiking adventure, the Dolomites offer countless opportunities to immerse yourself in the region's breathtaking natural beauty. By planning your journey thoughtfully and taking the time to savor the stunning vistas and unique experiences along the way, you'll be sure to leave the Dolomites with a deep appreciation for this truly remarkable corner of the world.

Guided nature tours

For those seeking to delve deeper into the Dolomites' remarkable flora, fauna, and geological formations, guided nature tours offer an unparalleled opportunity to connect with the region's natural heritage. Led by experienced naturalists and outdoors enthusiasts, these tours provide a comprehensive and insightful exploration of the Dolomites' most captivating natural wonders, allowing visitors to gain a greater understanding and appreciation for the delicate balance of this UNESCO World Heritage site.

Wildlife Watching Tours

A wide variety of wildlife can be found in the Dolomites, including the elusive Eurasian lynx, the swift chamois, and the majestic brown bear. Guided wildlife watching tours provide an opportunity for individuals who possess a strong fascination with these fascinating animals to observe them in their native environments and gain knowledge about their distinct habits and adaptations.

With a healthy population of brown bears, the Parco Naturale Adamello Brenta is one of the best places in the Dolomites to see wildlife. In this park, guided tours frequently include stops at designated bear observation areas where guests can safely watch these amazing animals playing, feeding, and caring for their young. With the help of naturalist guides, visitors can gain a deeper understanding of these magnificent alpine predators by learning in-depth details about the biology, habitat, and conservation efforts of bears.

Apart from brown bears, guided wildlife tours can also concentrate on seeing a variety of avian species like the colorful rock partridge and the majestic golden eagle, as well as other large mammals like the Eurasian lynx and ibex. Hiking through the pristine landscapes of the Dolomites is a common component of these tours, which helps visitors get closer to nature and raises their chances of seeing these elusive animals.

Botanical Hikes and Wildflower Walks

With more than 2,000 different species of vascular plants spread throughout the region's varied ecosystems, the Dolomites are a veritable botanical paradise. Naturalists who are passionate about the outdoors can discover the complex interactions between plants and their surroundings and the rich floral diversity of the Dolomites through guided botanical hikes and wildflower walks.

These specialized tours are usually offered in the spring and summer, when the alpine meadows and forests of the Dolomites are at their most beautiful. Along clearly designated trails, knowledgeable guides will lead guests through a diverse array of wildflowers, from the delicate edelweiss to the vivid arnica, pointing them out and identifying them while sharing information about their ecological significance, folklore, and adaptations.

These guided tours may cover the cultural heritage of the area and the traditional uses of various plants in local handicrafts, medicine, and cuisine, in addition to introducing visitors to the iconic and rare plant species of the Dolomites. The amalgamation of natural and cultural knowledge can significantly enhance a visitor's comprehension and admiration of the Dolomites' longstanding connection to the natural world.

Geological Exploration Tours
The striking limestone peaks and glacial formations of the Dolomites bear witness to the region's intriguing geological past, which has been molded by tectonic action, erosion, and climate change over millions of years. Visitors can explore the fascinating geologic history of the Dolomites and learn more about the processes that have shaped this distinctive landscape by taking guided geological exploration tours.

These trips frequently include visits to locations with special geological significance, like the Pale di San Martino massif, a towering limestone formation that is recognized as a UNESCO World Heritage site, or the Marmolada Glacier, the largest glacier in the Dolomites. A thorough explanation of the region's geological features, including the formation of the Dolomites' characteristic "pale" rock, the erosive power of glaciers, and the effects of climate change on the alpine environment, will be given by knowledgeable guides.

In order to give visitors a more comprehensive understanding of the processes that have shaped this remarkable landscape over time, many geological exploration tours also include hands-on activities like fossil hunting or rock identification workshops.

Whether you're interested in learning about the local geology, wildlife, or plants, guided nature tours in the Dolomites provide an interesting and rewarding way to experience the area's natural treasures. Through utilizing the knowledge and enthusiasm of the local guides, you will develop a fresh understanding of the delicate equilibrium and astounding variety of this UNESCO-protected mountain paradise.

CHAPTER 9.

GASTRONOMY IN THE DOLOMITES

Regional dishes and specialties

If you're lucky enough to be planning a trip to the Italian Dolomites, you're in for a true culinary adventure. This picturesque alpine region is renowned not only for its breathtaking natural beauty but also for its rich gastronomic heritage, which has been shaped by the interplay of local traditions, diverse cultural influences, and the bounty of the surrounding landscapes.

As you explore the charming villages and valleys of the Dolomites, you'll have the opportunity to indulge in a tantalizing array of regional dishes and specialties that showcase the best of local ingredients and time-honored cooking methods. From hearty, comforting fare to delicate, artisanal creations, the Dolomites' culinary offerings are sure to delight your palate and leave you with lasting memories of the region's unique flavors.

Canederli
Canederli, one of the Dolomites' most iconic regional dishes, are savory dumplings made with stale bread, eggs, milk, and a variety of fillings. These substantial, farm-style dumplings are a local cuisine staple and come in a variety of delectable flavors. A

traditional preparation is the "Tris di Canederli," or three-piece tasting, which may include versions stuffed with Speck (a type of cured ham unique to the South Tyrol region), spinach, or cheese. Dumplings are typically served in a rich, aromatic broth or with sauerkraut, resulting in a hearty and comforting meal that reflects the region's rustic, mountain-influenced culinary traditions.

Schlutzkrapfen

Schlutzkrapfen, a popular regional specialty, are delicate, half-moon-shaped pasta pockets filled with a variety of savory or sweet fillings. The most popular filling is a combination of ricotta, spinach, and Parmesan, which produces a rich, creamy, and slightly tangy flavor profile that complements the tender pasta dough. Schlutzkrapfen are typically served with a simple butter or sage sauce, which highlights the delicate flavors of the filling.

Gröstl

Gröstl is a flavorful pan-fried hash made with potatoes, onions, and various meats. The key to a great Gröstl is to carefully select and prepare the ingredients, which include crispy pan-fried potatoes and a variety of meats, such as smoky Speck or tender roast pork, combined with sautéed onions and a fragrant spice blend.

Strangolapreti

Strangolapreti, which translates to "priest stranglers," is a delicious pasta dish from the Dolomite region of Trentino-Alto Adige. These thick, chewy noodles are made from a simple dough of flour, eggs, and spinach, which results in a vibrant green color and a distinct earthy flavor. Strangolapreti are traditionally served with a rich, creamy sauce made of butter, Parmesan, and nutmeg, resulting in a harmonious and memorable dining experience.

Strudel

While not a traditional Dolomite dish, the delectable apple strudel is a popular and widespread treat throughout the region. This flaky, fruit-filled pastry has been a culinary staple in the Dolomites for generations, with local bakers and confectioners taking great pride in perfecting their recipes and methods. The key to a truly exceptional Dolomites strudel is the quality of the ingredients and the attention to detail in its preparation, which includes ripe, juicy apples wrapped in a delicate, paper-thin pastry dough.

Spätzle

Spätzle, a popular dish in the Dolomites and throughout the Alpine region, are small, fluffy egg noodles that are a versatile staple in local cuisine. These delicate dumplings can be served in a variety of ways, including tossed with butter and cheese or as a side dish alongside hearty meat-based dishes. Spätzle are typically made by hand, with the dough pressed through a special perforated tool to form the distinctive small, irregular shapes that define this traditional alpine specialty.

Käsespätzle

Based on the beloved Spätzle, Käsespätzle is a regional dish that elevates the noodles to new levels of indulgence. This dish combines fluffy Spätzle noodles with generous amounts of melted local cheeses like Bergkäse or Graukäse, resulting in a rich, creamy, and comforting meal that complements the Dolomites' rugged mountain landscapes.

Bombardino

While not a traditional regional dish, the Bombardino is a beloved and iconic Dolomites beverage that has evolved into a popular après-ski treat and a delightful way to warm up on a chilly alpine evening. This creamy, coffee-based cocktail combines egg liqueur, brandy or rum, and steamed milk to create a decadent and indulgent drink that perfectly captures the Dolomites' cozy, convivial spirit.

As you explore the charming villages and valleys of the Dolomites, be sure to try these regional dishes and specialties, which provide a delectable glimpse into the region's rich culinary heritage and the ingenuity of its local chefs. From hearty, comforting fare to delicate, artisanal creations, the Dolomites' culinary offerings will delight your palate and leave you with lasting memories of the region's distinct flavors.

Best restaurants and dining experiences

The Dolomites, with their stunning natural beauty and rich cultural heritage, have long been a draw for discerning travelers seeking not only breathtaking landscapes but also a culinary adventure. Fortunately, the region is home to a wealth of exceptional restaurants and dining experiences that showcase the very best of local ingredients, traditional recipes, and innovative culinary talents.

Hotel La Perla, Corvara

Nestled in the charming alpine village of Corvara, the Hotel La Perla is a beloved destination for both our guides and longtime clients, and it's easy to see why. The hotel is home to the acclaimed Michelin-starred chef Nicola Laera, whose culinary prowess has earned her a reputation as a true innovator in northern Italian cuisine.

Nicola's menus masterfully blend traditional Ladin (the local Romance language) cooking techniques and flavors with modern influences, resulting in dishes that are both deeply rooted in the region's culinary heritage and infused with a forward-thinking, creative spirit. Standout items include her risotto, served with apple and oysters, as well as the succulent belly of lamb, sourced from a neighboring valley and paired with pine nuts and locally foraged mushrooms.

Whether you're dining in the hotel's main restaurant or one of its more intimate, specialized venues, you'll be treated to an exceptional gastronomic experience that showcases the Dolomites' bounty in the most elevated and captivating way.

Rifugio Averau, Cortina d'Ampezzo

Rifugio Averau offers a truly immersive dining experience that highlights the Dolomites' magnificent natural surroundings. Perched at an altitude of 2,413 meters (7,913 feet) in the heart of the Cortina d'Ampezzo region, this mountain refuge offers panoramic views of the towering Nuvolau Group and Cinque Torri peaks, creating a breathtaking backdrop for your culinary journey.

The Rifugio Averau's menu demonstrates the region's commitment to sustainability and the use of locally sourced ingredients. Dishes like the hearty Ladin-style barley soup, the tender venison stew, and the decadent apple strudel demonstrate the kitchen's mastery of traditional alpine cuisine while also highlighting the abundance of produce and meats from the surrounding pastures and forests.

What distinguishes a meal at the Rifugio Averau is the opportunity to savor these exceptional dishes while surrounded by the Dolomites' majestic peaks and serene, high-altitude landscapes. It's a dining experience that seamlessly combines the region's culinary and natural wonders, leaving a lasting impression on the senses.

Restaurant Laurin, Brunico

The Restaurant Laurin, located in the picturesque town of Brunico, has long been a shining example of culinary excellence in the Dolomites, earning a well-deserved reputation for its innovative take on traditional South Tyrolean cuisine.

The Laurin's menu, overseen by head chef Andreas Zugna, is a harmonious fusion of traditional regional dishes and cutting-edge culinary techniques. Standout dishes include tender, slow-cooked pork cheek with Spätzle and a vibrant, herb-forward salad, as well as delicate ravioli filled with ricotta and spinach and served in a delicate butter-sage sauce.

What truly distinguishes the Laurin is its unwavering dedication to sourcing the best local ingredients, from the succulent meats and cheeses of South Tyrol to the freshest seasonal produce foraged from the surrounding meadows and forests. This commitment to quality and provenance is evident in every bite, making the Laurin a must-see destination for discerning foodies looking to immerse themselves in the Dolomites' culinary magic.

Ristorante Tivoli, Cortina d'Ampezzo

For an elegant and refined dining experience that captures the sophisticated spirit of the Dolomites, Cortina d'Ampezzo's Ristorante Tivoli is a must-visit. The Tivoli, located within the historic Hotel Villa Oretta, provides a truly unforgettable gastronomic journey that seamlessly blends traditional regional flavors with modern, internationally inspired culinary techniques.

The menu, created by talented chef Mauro Taufer, reflects the Dolomites' diverse culinary influences, featuring dishes inspired by the region's Ladin, Austrian, and Italian roots. Delicate spaghetti with local mountain cheeses and black truffle, perfectly cooked rack of lamb with roasted vegetables, and decadent chocolate mousse with a hint of orange are among the standouts.

What distinguishes Ristorante Tivoli is its dedication to providing a truly immersive dining experience, complete with impeccable service, a carefully curated wine list, and a sophisticated yet inviting ambiance that complements the culinary artistry on display. Whether you're looking for a romantic evening out or a celebratory meal, the Tivoli is a must-see destination for those seeking the best in Dolomites dining.

Ristorante Siriola, San Cassiano

Ristorante Siriola, located in the charming village of San Cassiano, has long been a beacon of culinary excellence in the Dolomites, earning a well-deserved Michelin star for its unwavering commitment to showcasing the region's finest ingredients and time-honored cooking techniques.

The Siriola's menu, led by chef Matteo Metullio, is a veritable symphony of flavors, with each dish carefully crafted to combine traditional Ladin and South Tyrolean influences with modern, globally inspired culinary flourishes. Standout dishes include delicate ravioli filled with mountain cheese and pine nuts, tender venison with a rich juniper and berry sauce, and decadent Sacher torte with a hint of local mountain honey.

What truly distinguishes Ristorante Siriola is its dedication to sustainability and the preservation of the Dolomites' culinary heritage. From sourcing the freshest local produce to honoring the region's time-honored cooking methods, the Siriola team is deeply committed to celebrating the Dolomites' bounty in the most elevated and captivating way possible.

Malga Panna, Moena.
Visit Malga Panna in the charming town of Moena for a truly immersive and authentic dining experience that celebrates the pastoral heritage of the Dolomites. This traditional mountain hut, perched amidst the region's lush alpine meadows, provides a glimpse into the centuries-old traditions of Ladin mountain cuisine, with a menu featuring the best locally sourced ingredients and time-honored cooking methods.

The star of the show at Malga Panna is undoubtedly the exceptional artisanal cheeses, which are made on-site with milk from the herd of cows that graze the surrounding pastures. These rich, flavorful cheeses are featured in a variety of dishes, ranging from classic Ladin-style barley soup to decadent raclette platters, giving guests a true taste of the Dolomites' pastoral heritage.

Aside from the exceptional cheese, Malga Panna's menu includes other regional specialties like the hearty Gröstl (a mountain-style hash), tender venison stew, and irresistible apple strudel. Dining at Malga Panna is more than just a meal; it's a cultural immersion that connects visitors to the Dolomites' deep-rooted traditions and the hardworking mountain communities that have shaped this remarkable region over generations.

Ristorante Dolada, Pieve di Cadore
Ristorante Dolada, located in the picturesque town of Pieve di Cadore, is a true hidden gem that provides a dining experience that seamlessly blends the natural beauty of the Dolomites with its rich culinary heritage. The Dolada's menu, led by chef Nicola Del Mestre, celebrates the region's finest seasonal ingredients, expertly

crafted into dishes that capture the essence of Ladin and South Tyrolean cuisines.

The Dolada's menu features delicate ravioli filled with local cheeses and herbs, tender venison with a rich, berry-infused sauce, and decadent apple strudel with a delightful hint of cinnamon. What truly distinguishes the Dolada is its dedication to sustainability and the preservation of the Dolomites' culinary heritage, with the team sourcing the majority of their ingredients from local producers and purveyors.

Dining at the Ristorante Dolada is more than just a meal; it's an opportunity to immerse yourself in the Dolomites' rich cultural tapestry, with each bite telling a story about the region's history, natural bounty, and the hardworking people who have shaped its culinary identity over time.

Whether you're looking for Michelin-starred excellence, traditional mountain hut fare, or innovative, regionally inspired cuisine, the Dolomites have a plethora of exceptional dining experiences that will leave an indelible impression on your palate and heart. By indulging in these culinary gems, you'll not only savor the region's flavors, but also gain a better understanding of the Dolomites' remarkable natural and cultural heritage.

Food and wine tours

The Dolomites region of northern Italy is a true paradise for food and wine enthusiasts, offering a diverse array of immersive experiences that allow visitors to delve deep into the rich culinary heritage and terroir of this remarkable alpine landscape. From guided tastings of locally produced wines and cheeses to hands-on cooking classes and foraging expeditions, the Dolomites provide countless opportunities to savor the flavors that have sustained the local communities for generations.

Dolomites Wine and Cheese Tasting Tour
A guided wine and cheese tasting tour is essential for learning about the Dolomites' renowned viticulture and artisanal cheese-making traditions. These specialized excursions take visitors behind the scenes, introducing them to the passionate producers and family-owned farms that form the foundation of the region's culinary identity.

During these immersive experiences, guests will be able to sample a wide range of locally crafted wines, from the crisp, aromatic whites of the Alto Adige region to the bold, structured reds that thrive in Trentino. Equally enthralling are the Dolomites' world-class cheeses, which range from the rich, creamy Alpines to the bold, pungent mountain varieties, each with its own distinct flavor profile shaped by the region's distinct terrain.

Beyond simply tasting these exceptional products, the tour guides provide insightful information about the production methods, regional traditions, and sustainability practices that support the Dolomites' thriving food and wine culture. This holistic approach not only pleases the palate but also fosters a greater appreciation for the region's culinary heritage.

Foraging and Cooking Experiences

For a truly immersive culinary adventure in the Dolomites, consider a foraging and cooking experience that allows you to connect with the land and its bounty. These guided expeditions take participants into the region's lush alpine meadows, dense forests, and hidden valleys, where they will learn to identify and harvest a wide variety of wild edibles, including fragrant herbs, vibrant wildflowers, succulent mushrooms, and tart berries.

Foragers will not only discover the Dolomites' wealth of natural resources, but will also learn traditional preservation and preparation techniques passed down through generations. Armed with their foraged finds, participants return to the kitchen to prepare a variety of delectable dishes that highlight the purity and seasonality of the region's ingredients.

These immersive cooking classes offer a unique opportunity to learn about the Dolomites' culinary traditions, as participants prepare classic regional specialties such as Canederli (savory bread dumplings) and Strangolapreti (handmade spinach pasta) using the same methods and ingredients that have defined the area's gastronomic identity for centuries.

Distillery and Liqueur Tastings

In addition to its well-known wines and cheeses, the Dolomites region is home to a thriving culture of artisanal distilleries and liqueur producers, each with their own distinct recipes and production methods based on the area's rich history and natural resources.

Visitors to the Dolomites can discover this fascinating aspect of the region's culinary heritage through guided tastings and behind-the-scenes tours of local distilleries. These experiences provide a detailed look at the production of traditional mountain spirits like the herbaceous Grappa and the rich, fragrant Bombardino (a creamy, coffee-based liqueur that has become a popular après-ski treat).

In addition to the opportunity to sample these unique libations, distillery tours offer valuable insights into the region's foraging traditions, as many producers use locally harvested botanicals, fruits, and herbs in their small-batch creations. This holistic approach not only produces exceptional products, but it also protects the Dolomites' centuries-old culinary heritage.

Whether you're a seasoned oenophile, a cheese connoisseur, or simply someone who appreciates the distinct flavors of a particular region, the Dolomites provide a plethora of immersive food and wine experiences that will leave an indelible mark on your palate and understanding of this magnificent alpine landscape.

Farmers' markets and local producers

The Dolomites region of northern Italy is a veritable treasure trove for food-loving travelers, with a vibrant network of farmers' markets and local producers that offer unparalleled opportunities to immerse oneself in the region's rich culinary heritage. From bustling town squares to quaint mountain villages, these vibrant hubs of local commerce and community showcase the very best of the Dolomites' seasonal bounty and time-honored artisanal traditions.

Bolzano Farmers' Market, Bolzano

The Bolzano Farmers' Market, located in the heart of the Alto Adige region, is a must-see destination for anyone looking to reconnect with the Dolomites' agricultural roots. Every Saturday morning in the historic Piazza Walther, this vibrant market is a sensory feast, with row after row of stalls brimming with the freshest local produce, artisanal cheeses, and cured meats.

What distinguishes the Bolzano Farmers' Market is its unwavering dedication to highlighting the region's small-scale, family-owned farms and producers, many of whom have been supplying the community for generations. Visitors can expect to find an exceptional assortment of crisp, aromatic apples and pears, earthy mountain potatoes, and an impressive selection of Speck (a regional specialty of cured, smoked ham).

In addition to the exceptional produce, the Bolzano Farmers' Market offers a wide variety of specialty food items, including fragrant honeys and handcrafted jams, as well as artisanal breads and pastries. It's the ideal spot to put together a picnic of locally sourced delicacies to enjoy amidst the Dolomites' breathtaking scenery.

Farmers' Market in Cortina d'Ampezzo.
Nestled in the heart of the Dolomites' most iconic ski resort town, the Cortina d'Ampezzo Farmers' Market is a must-see for anyone looking for a true taste of the region's culinary heritage. This vibrant market, held every Wednesday and Saturday throughout the summer, highlights the exceptional bounty of the surrounding valleys and alpine meadows.

One of the most notable aspects of the Cortina d'Ampezzo Farmers' Market is its emphasis on traditional, sustainable farming practices and the preservation of local food cultures. Visitors can expect to find an impressive selection of artisanal cheeses, ranging from the rich, creamy Alpines to the bold, pungent mountain varieties, all made using time-honored methods by dedicated cheesemakers.

In addition to the exceptional dairy products, the Cortina d'Ampezzo Farmers' Market provides a plethora of other locally sourced delicacies, such as freshly baked breads, seasonal produce, and a variety of preserves, honeys, and specialty items. It's the ideal place to immerse oneself in the Dolomites' rich culinary heritage and meet the passionate producers who protect the region's gastronomic identity.

Moena Farmers' Market, Moena

Nestled in the heart of the Trentino region, the charming town of Moena hosts a vibrant farmers' market that highlights the exceptional quality and diversity of the Dolomites' agricultural bounty. This vibrant market, held every Saturday morning in the town's central piazza, is a must-see for anyone looking to experience the region's deep ties to the land and its seasonal rhythms.

One of the most notable aspects of the Moena Farmers' Market is its emphasis on traditional, sustainable farming practices and the preservation of local food cultures. Visitors can expect to find an impressive variety of locally grown produce, ranging from crisp, fragrant greens and vibrant berries in the summer to hearty root vegetables and winter squashes that thrive in the alpine environment.

Aside from the exceptional produce, the Moena Farmers' Market offers a wide range of other locally sourced delicacies, such as handcrafted cheeses, cured meats, and a variety of preserves, honeys, and other specialty items. It's the ideal location to put together a picnic of Dolomites-sourced delicacies to enjoy while exploring the region's breathtaking scenery.

Canazei Farmers' Market, Canazei

The charming town of Canazei, located in the heart of the Fassa Valley, hosts a vibrant farmers' market that provides a unique and immersive glimpse into the Dolomites' rich agricultural heritage. Taking place every Wednesday and Saturday during the summer, this lively market is a true celebration of the region's seasonal bounty and the hardworking producers who cultivate it.

One of the Canazei Farmers' Market's distinguishing features is its emphasis on traditional, small-scale farming practices and the preservation of the Dolomites' Ladin culinary traditions. Visitors can expect to find an exceptional variety of locally grown produce, from crisp, earthy potatoes and fragrant herbs in the summer to hearty root vegetables and winter squashes that thrive in the alpine environment.

In addition to the exceptional produce, the Canazei Farmers' Market offers a variety of other locally sourced delicacies, such as handcrafted cheeses, cured meats, preserves, honeys, and other specialty items. It's the ideal place to immerse oneself in the Dolomites' rich culinary heritage and meet the passionate producers who protect the region's gastronomic identity.

Agordo Farmers' Market, Agordo

Nestled in the picturesque Agordo Valley, the Agordo Farmers' Market is a hidden gem that provides a one-of-a-kind and intimate glimpse into the Dolomites' artisanal culinary culture. Every Saturday morning in the town's central piazza, this bustling market is a true celebration of the region's small-scale producers and the exceptional quality of their products.

One of the Agordo Farmers' Market's distinguishing features is its emphasis on traditional, family-owned farms and the preservation of heirloom fruits, vegetables, and grains. Visitors can expect to find a variety of unusual and difficult-to-find produce, ranging from vibrant, heritage-breed tomatoes to earthy, nutrient-dense mountain greens that thrive in the Dolomites' harsh alpine climate.

In addition to the exceptional produce, the Agordo Farmers' Market offers a wide range of other locally sourced delicacies, such as artisanal cheeses, cured meats, and a variety of preserves, honeys, and other specialty items. It's the ideal place to meet the passionate producers who are the stewards of the Dolomites' culinary heritage and put together a picnic of truly exceptional, locally sourced ingredients.

Whether you want to immerse yourself in the Dolomites' vibrant food culture, meet the hardworking producers who shape its gastronomic identity, or simply put together a picnic of exceptional, locally sourced ingredients, the region's farmers' markets and local producers provide an unparalleled opportunity to savor the flavors of this remarkable alpine landscape.

CHAPTER 10.

PRACTICAL INFORMATION FOR VISITORS

Language and communication

The Dolomites region is a true linguistic tapestry, with a diverse array of languages and dialects that reflect the area's rich cultural heritage. As a visitor, understanding the local linguistic landscape can greatly enhance your experience and help you communicate more effectively with the friendly and welcoming people of the Dolomites.

The primary languages spoken in the Dolomites are Italian and German, with the latter being the dominant language in the region's northern reaches, particularly in Alto Adige (or South Tyrol). This linguistic divide is a result of the region's history, as the Dolomites were once part of the Austro-Hungarian Empire before joining Italy following World War I.

In addition to Italian and German, the Dolomites are home to the Ladin language, a Romance language closely related to Romansh that is spoken by a small but thriving minority population in the region's central and eastern valleys. Ladin has a rich cultural heritage and is widely recognized as an essential component of the Dolomites' distinct identity.

As you explore the Dolomites, you'll notice that many locals, particularly those in the tourism industry, speak English fluently, making it easy to get by without knowing Italian or German. However, learning a few basic phrases in the local languages can help you connect with people and improve your overall experience.

Some essential Italian phrases to know include:

- "Buongiorno" (Good morning)
- "Buonasera" (Good evening)
- "Per favore" (Please)
- "Grazie" (Thank you)
- "Parla inglese?" (Do you speak English?)

For those venturing into the more German-speaking areas of the Dolomites, familiarizing yourself with some basic German phrases can be incredibly helpful:

- "Guten Tag" (Good day)
- "Bitte" (Please)
- "Danke" (Thank you)
- "Sprichst du Englisch?" (Do you speak English?)

Additionally, if you plan to explore the Ladin-speaking regions, a few simple Ladin phrases can go a long way in connecting with the local community:

- "Bun dé" (Good day)
- "Grass" (Thank you)
- "Co stès?" (How are you?)

Keep in mind that, while many locals, particularly in tourist-oriented areas, will be able to communicate in English, making an effort to learn a few words and phrases in the local languages can be a thoughtful gesture that the people of the Dolomites will appreciate.

Beyond spoken communication, it's critical to become acquainted with the written signage and wayfinding systems you'll encounter throughout the area. Road signs, trail markers, and other public information are frequently displayed in multiple languages, including Italian, German, and Ladin, so knowing how to recognize and navigate these multilingual systems can greatly improve your ability to explore the Dolomites with confidence.

You will enhance your communication abilities and obtain a deeper comprehension of the rich cultural legacy that characterizes this exceptional alpine region by embracing the linguistic diversity of the Dolomites and actively engaging in the local languages. So, knowing a little bit of the local language can make your time in the Dolomites truly unforgettable and immersive, whether you're ordering a traditional Ladin dish, asking for directions to a trailhead, or just saying hello to the people.

Currency and banking

When visiting the Dolomites region of northern Italy, it's important for travelers to be well-versed in the local currency and banking practices to ensure a seamless and stress-free experience. Understanding the nuances of currency exchange, accessing funds, and managing your finances can go a long way in helping you make the most of your time in this breathtaking alpine paradise.

Currency

The Euro (€) is the official currency of the Dolomites and Italy as a whole. This European Union-wide currency is widely accepted throughout the region, making it the preferred method of payment for purchases, services, and transactions.

It's worth noting that many businesses, particularly those catering to tourists, may accept other major currencies, such as the US Dollar or the British Pound, but the exchange rate and potential fees can make these less appealing options. Carrying and using Euros is generally recommended for the best value and convenience while visiting the Dolomites.

Banking and ATM

The Dolomites region has a well-developed banking infrastructure, including a network of ATMs (known locally as "Bancomat") spread across the towns and villages. These ATMs are widely available and allow you to withdraw Euros from your home bank account, often at better exchange rates than currency exchange bureaus.

When using ATMs in the Dolomites, notify your bank of your travel plans to avoid any potential issues with your card being flagged as suspicious activity. It's also a good idea to have a backup payment method, such as a second debit or credit card, in case your primary card experiences any unforeseen problems.

Many banks in the Dolomites provide currency exchange services, usually at major branch locations or airports. While these can be convenient options, it is critical to shop around and compare exchange rates, as some may provide less favorable terms than using your home bank's ATM or a dedicated currency exchange facility.

Credit and Debit Cards

Credit and debit cards are widely accepted in the Dolomites, especially at larger hotels, restaurants, and retail establishments. Visa, Mastercard, and American Express are the most widely accepted credit card networks in the region.

When using your cards, notify your issuer of your travel plans to avoid potential fraud detection issues. It's also a good idea to learn about any foreign transaction fees or currency conversion charges that may apply to your specific card, as these can affect the total cost of your purchases.

In more remote or rural areas of the Dolomites, cash may be the preferred method of payment, so keep some Euros on hand for smaller transactions and incidentals.

You can ensure a hassle-free and financially savvy experience while exploring the Dolomites by becoming acquainted with the local currency, banking, and payment options. Remember to plan ahead of time, communicate with your financial institutions, and be prepared to use a variety of payment methods to make the most of your time in this extraordinary corner of Italy.

Health and safety considerations

As you prepare to embark on your journey to the Dolomites, it's essential to consider the unique health and safety considerations of this breathtaking alpine region. By familiarizing yourself with the local resources and best practices, you can ensure a safe and enjoyable experience as you explore the stunning landscapes and immerse yourself in the rich cultural heritage of this remarkable corner of Italy.

Medical Facilities and Emergencies

The Dolomites region has a well-developed network of modern medical facilities and emergency services to meet the needs of both residents and tourists. Major towns and cities, including Bolzano, Cortina d'Ampezzo, and Trento, have well-equipped hospitals and clinics that offer a wide range of medical services, from routine check-ups to emergency treatments.

In the event of a medical emergency, dial the European emergency number, 112, which will connect you to the appropriate emergency services, such as ambulance, fire, or police, depending on the situation. It's worth noting that, while many medical professionals in the Dolomites speak English well, it's a good idea to become acquainted with key Italian medical terminology or keep a translation app on hand to facilitate effective communication.

Altitude and Acclimatization

One of the most important health considerations when visiting the Dolomites is the high altitude. With peaks reaching over 3,000 meters (9,800 feet), the higher elevation can increase the risk of altitude sickness, especially for those who are not used to such environments.

To reduce the effects of altitude, it is recommended that you gradually acclimate to higher elevations by spending a few days at lower altitudes before ascending. Staying hydrated, avoiding strenuous activities, and being aware of the symptoms of altitude sickness (headache, nausea, dizziness) can all contribute to a safe and comfortable experience.

If you notice signs of altitude sickness, you should descend to a lower elevation and seek medical attention if the symptoms persist or worsen.

Environmental Hazards and Safety.

The Dolomites' rugged, mountainous terrain and changing weather conditions present a number of environmental risks that visitors should be aware of and prepared for.

Proper hiking gear, such as sturdy footwear, warm layers, and rain protection, is required for navigating the region's trails while remaining comfortable and safe. Before starting your hikes, make sure to check trail conditions, weather forecasts, and any potential hazards, such as avalanche risks.

In addition to being prepared for the physical environment, it is critical to be aware of your personal safety while exploring the Dolomites. Familiarize yourself with local emergency contacts, keep your belongings safe, and exercise caution when traveling to more remote or isolated areas.

You can reduce the risks and maximize the enjoyment of your Dolomites adventure by staying informed, packing the necessary gear, and taking prudent safety precautions.

Remember that your health and well-being should be your top priorities as you explore the breathtaking landscapes and rich cultural tapestry of this remarkable alpine region.

Local etiquette and customs

As you prepare to explore the stunning Dolomites region of northern Italy, it's important to familiarize yourself with the local etiquette and customs to ensure a respectful and culturally enriching experience. By understanding and embracing the nuances of the region's social norms, you can forge deeper connections with the welcoming local communities and fully immerse yourself in the unique heritage and traditions that define this remarkable alpine landscape.

Greetings and Introductions
In the Dolomites, a warm and courteous greeting is highly valued. When meeting someone for the first time, the customary greeting is "Buongiorno" (Good morning) or "Buonasera" (Good evening), followed by a friendly smile and a handshake.

It is also polite to introduce yourself by stating your name, and you may be asked for additional information, such as where you are from or why you are visiting. Respond with a similar level of warmth and openness to demonstrate your willingness to engage with the local community.

Dining and Meal Times
Mealtimes in the Dolomites are often regarded as sacred social rituals, and it is critical to follow local customs and etiquette while dining.

When dining in a restaurant, it is polite to wait to be seated by the staff, and once seated, do not begin your meal until the entire table has been served. It is also customary to wait until the host or the eldest person at the table starts eating before beginning your own meal.

It is considered respectful to keep your elbows off the table and to avoid rushed or hurried eating. Savoring the flavors and conversing with your dining companions is highly valued in the Dolomite culinary culture.

When it's time to leave, a simple "Grazie, buon appetito" (Thank you, enjoy your meal) is a polite way to show your gratitude.

Tipping and Service Charges
Tipping customs in the Dolomites vary, but in general, a 10-15% tip is considered appropriate for good service in restaurants, taxis, and other service-based businesses.

It's worth noting that many restaurants in the region may already include a service charge, known as a "coperto," on the bill, which usually ranges between 1-3 euros per person. In these cases, an additional tip is not required, but a small token of appreciation is always appreciated.

Environmental consciousness and sustainability.
The Dolomites are famous for their breathtaking natural beauty and the locals' dedication to environmental stewardship. As a visitor, you should show respect for the region's fragile ecosystems and sustainable practices.

This could include properly disposing of waste, avoiding single-use plastics, and being conscious of your water and energy consumption. It is also advisable to stick to marked trails and avoid disturbing the local flora and fauna.

By adopting the Dolomites' local etiquette and customs, you will not only show respect for the region's cultural heritage, but you will also improve your overall experience. From polite greetings and dining etiquette to environmental awareness and sustainable practices, the friendly people of the Dolomites will appreciate your willingness to adapt to the local way of life.

Transportation within the Dolomites

Exploring the stunning landscapes of the Dolomites requires a reliable and efficient transportation network, and as a visitor, familiarizing yourself with the various transportation options available can greatly enhance your experience in this remarkable alpine region.

Public Transportation
The Dolomites region has a well-developed public transportation system, making it both convenient and environmentally friendly.
Buses: The Dolomites have a vast network of regional and local bus lines connecting the major towns and villages. These buses are frequently outfitted with bike racks, making them a convenient option for those looking to incorporate hiking or cycling into their itinerary. Purchasing a multi-day bus pass can help you save money and have more flexibility during your stay.

Trains: For longer journeys within the Dolomites, the region's train system is a dependable and comfortable option. The main train lines, such as the Brenner Railway, connect the Dolomites to the rest of Italy and beyond, providing seamless connections for visitors arriving from other locations.

Taxi and Rideshare Services

Taxis are widely available in the Dolomites' larger towns and cities, making it easy to navigate urban areas or travel to more remote locations. It is best to agree on a fare with the driver before embarking on your journey, as metered rates can vary.

Furthermore, ridesharing services such as Uber and locally-based options are gaining popularity in the Dolomites, providing an alternative to traditional taxis, particularly for shorter trips or shared rides.

Private Transportation

For those who prefer the flexibility and independence of private transportation, the Dolomites offer several options to consider:

Rental Cars: Renting a car can be a great way to explore the region at your own pace, allowing you to visit remote villages, hiking trails, and scenic viewpoints that are difficult to reach by public transportation. Before you set out, make sure you are familiar with the local driving customs and regulations.

Motorcycles and Scooters: For an exciting and environmentally friendly mode of transportation, rent a motorcycle or scooter and explore the Dolomites' winding mountain roads and picturesque towns. This option is especially popular with adventurous travelers and offers a unique perspective on the region.

Trekking and Hiking

For those who wish to fully immerse themselves in the natural beauty of the Dolomites, trekking and hiking are among the most rewarding ways to explore the region. The Dolomites boast an extensive network of well-maintained trails, ranging from easy strolls to challenging multi-day hikes, that connect the various towns and villages.

When planning your hiking trips, make sure to research trail conditions, difficulty levels, and any required permits or fees. It's also important to bring the right gear, such as sturdy hiking boots, weather-appropriate clothing, and emergency supplies.

You can maximize your visit and fully experience the breathtaking landscapes and lively local communities by familiarizing yourself with the Dolomites' varied transportation options. This will help you navigate this breathtaking alpine region with ease and efficiency.

Tips for first-time visitors

As you prepare to embark on your first journey to the Dolomites, a remarkable alpine region in northern Italy, it's essential to arm yourself with a wealth of practical knowledge to ensure a truly memorable and enriching experience. Drawing from our extensive research, local insights, and experience, we've compiled a comprehensive set of tips to help first-time visitors make the most of their time in this stunning corner of the world.

Plan Ahead and Pack Wisely

The Dolomites are a vast and diverse region, so plan your itinerary ahead of time. Research must-see destinations, popular hiking trails, and cultural events to create a well-balanced and engaging itinerary tailored to your preferences. Also, be aware of the region's seasonal variations, as weather conditions can have a significant impact on accessibility and activities.

Consider the diverse climate and terrain of the Dolomites when packing for your adventure. Bring layers of warm, moisture-wicking clothing, sturdy hiking boots, rain gear, and sunscreen. Don't forget to bring any medications, a first-aid kit, and any specialized equipment you may require for your planned activities, such as trekking poles or climbing gear.

Embrace the Linguistic Diversity

The Dolomites are a linguistic tapestry, with Italian, German, and the minority Ladin languages all contributing significantly to the region's cultural heritage. While many locals, particularly in tourist-oriented areas, speak English fluently, learning a few basic phrases in the local languages can greatly improve your interactions and connections with the friendly people of the Dolomites.

Start with simple greetings, such as "Buongiorno" (Italian), "Guten Tag" (German), and "Bun dé" (Ladin), as well as expressions of gratitude like "Grazie" and "Danke." These small gestures will be greatly appreciated and can open the door to more meaningful exchanges.

Prioritize Health and Safety

The Dolomites' high elevation and rugged terrain necessitate a greater awareness of potential health and safety risks. Familiarize yourself with the symptoms of altitude sickness and take the necessary precautions, such as gradually adjusting to higher elevations. Before your trip, make sure to check the availability of medical facilities, emergency services, and any necessary vaccinations or health advisories.

When exploring the Dolomites' hiking trails and outdoor activities, make sure to pack the right gear, check the weather forecast, and stick to marked paths. Inform others about your hiking plans and bring necessary safety equipment, such as a map, compass, and emergency supplies.

Immerse yourself in local culture.

The Dolomites are known for their rich cultural heritage, which is deeply ingrained in the daily lives of the locals. Take the time to interact with the locals, sample traditional cuisine, and visit historical sites and cultural events. This immersive approach will not only increase your appreciation for the Dolomites, but will also help you form meaningful connections with the friendly locals.

Consider attending a local festival, visiting a traditional mountain hut (rifugio), or taking a cooking class to gain a better understanding of the Dolomites' distinct cultural tapestry.

Embrace Sustainable and Eco-Friendly Practices

The Dolomites are a natural wonderland, and the local communities are deeply committed to environmental stewardship. As a visitor, it's essential to adopt sustainable and eco-friendly practices to minimize your impact on this fragile alpine ecosystem.

This could include properly disposing of waste, avoiding single-use plastics, and being aware of your water and energy consumption. When hiking, follow marked trails and avoid disturbing the local flora and fauna.

By following these comprehensive tips, first-time visitors to the Dolomites will be well-prepared to confidently navigate this stunning alpine region, immerse themselves in local culture, and have a truly unforgettable and enriching experience.